WORLD RELIGIONS

WORLD RELIGIONS

Myrtle Langley

A LION MANUAL
Oxford · Batavia · Sydney

Published by
Lion Publishing plc
Sandy Lane West, Oxford, England
ISBN 0 7459 2541 3
Lion Publishing
1705 Hubbard Avenue, Batavia,
Illinois 60510, USA
ISBN 0 7459 2541 3
Albatross Books Pty Ltd
PO Box 320, Sutherland, NSW 2232, Australia
ISBN 0 7324 0761 3

First edition 1993

A catalogue record for this book is available
from the British Library

**Library of Congress Cataloging-in-
Publication Data**
Langley, Myrtle.
    World Religions/Myrtle Langley.
    "A Lion Manual"—Cover.
    ISBN 0-7459-2541-3
    1. Religions–Handbooks, manuals, etc.
I. Title.
BL82.L33 1993   93-4038
291—dc20 CIP

Printed and bound in Slovenia

Acknowledgments
Photographs by Fritz Fankhauser: pages
16–17; Hutchison: pages 27, 40, 52, 53, 59, 71,
74, 84, 88, 92; /Christina Dodwell: page 12;
/Michael Macintyre: pages 18, 44 (bottom), 45;
/Christine Pemberton: pages 23, 50, 62;
/Jeremy A. Homer: page 29; /Alex Stuart:
pages 30–31; /Lucie Motion: page 32; /R. Ian
Lloyd: pages 34, 88–89; /Trevor Page: pages
36, 61; /Sarah Errington: page 41 (bottom);
/S. Burman: page 47; /John Hatt: page 49;
Peter Stiles: page 76; Lion Publishing: pages 64,
83; /David Alexander: pages 67, 73; Topham:
pages 15, 20–21, 24, 38–39, 41 (top), 44 (top),
80–81, 87, 93; /Associated Press: pages 54, 91;
/C. Osborne: page 57; Zefa: page 69

CONTENTS

INTRODUCTION

This is a brief illustrated introduction to the world's greatest religions. I have tried to present the essence of a large and complex subject as interestingly, as simply, and as concisely as possible. The task has been both fascinating and rewarding.

For those of you who require some idea of what religion is and how I approach the subject, there is a short introductory chapter. It may well not be of interest to everyone. You may wish to skim through it quickly, returning to it later. For those who are curious to know what I believe and why, there is a short epilogue. I am both by circumstances of birth and conscious choice unashamedly a follower of Jesus Christ, finding him to be without equal and beyond compare.

Having said this, I must add that I deeply respect the longings and aspirations of the founders and followers of the world's great religions. I seek to treat each religion fairly and with sympathy, letting each speak for itself and making no attempt either to interpret or to compare.

Myrtle S. Langley

WHAT IS RELIGION?

Studying religion

No definition of religion can be entirely adequate. The Latin *religio*, from which our English word comes, originally meant reverence for the gods, or simply superstition. But it certainly means much more than that. It is helpful to look at any religion in terms of several aspects or 'dimensions', which concern the beliefs of the religion, its practices and the way it affects the individual and society.

Religion has at least six dimensions. Which dimension we place first depends on whether we see religion primarily as what people believe or as what they do. Westerners tend to emphasize beliefs. But, a 'religious person' is still thought of as someone who practises religion.

What is religion?

'Religion' is the response of human beings to the human condition. Faced with the difficulties of living in this world, we develop an

Two traditions

This study of religions makes no attempt to draw comparisons. But there is one distinction which is helpful to point out. The world's religions broadly divide into two very different groups: the Western prophetic tradition and the Eastern salvationist or mystical tradition.

The Western tradition

Springs from a parent Semitic group.

Includes Judaism, Christianity, Islam and their offshoots.

Prophetic, emphasizing the revelation of God to humans from outside the human spirit.

'World-affirming', accepting the essential goodness of the physical, and seeking the redemption or transformation of this sinful world.

The Eastern tradition

Springs from a parent Indian root.

Includes Hinduism, Buddhism and their offshoots.

Mystical, emphasizing the finding of God by humans from within the human spirit.

'World-denying', accepting the essentially spiritual nature of reality, and seeking release for the soul from the endless round of rebirth or reincarnation to which it is subjected in this world.

Six dimensions

Religion has been looked at in at least six dimensions.

Doctrine A belief system which gives a total explanation of reality.

Myth Stories about God and the gods, creation and salvation, and events of historical significance. (Myth is not the same as fiction.)

Ethics Values and codes of behaviour.

Ritual Worship, festivals, 'rites of passage' and initiations, and customs regulating food and dress.

Experience The individual's experience of the awe-inspiring and the transcendent, or a sense of belonging and commitment to something greater than the self.

Social The institutional organization of people to practise their religion.

as humankind's best argument for the existence of God. Augustine saw this in what he called our 'restlessness of heart'. Rudolf Otto saw it in the 'sense of the awe-inspiring', the 'numinous'.

understanding of our universe and our existence, so that life takes on purpose and significance.

To some people, religion is 'true' simply in terms of its usefulness. Emile Durkheim, the founder of modern sociology, considered that religion performed an essential function in society. Others, looking at religion in terms of its origins, say that it is nothing more than an escape-fantasy. Freud called it 'an illusion'. Karl Marx called it 'a sigh of oppression'.

To others again, religion is seen

'Religion is...'

Religion is 'the flight of the alone to the Alone'.
PLOTINUS

Religion is 'what a man does with his solitariness'.
A.N. WHITEHEAD

'Men create the gods in their own image.'
XENOPHANES

'One religion is as true as another.'
ROBERT BURTON

'We must have religion for religion's sake . . .'
VICTOR COUSIN

'You have created us for yourself, and our heart is restless until it comes to rest in you.'
AUGUSTINE OF HIPPO (354–430), THE GREAT LEADER OF THE EARLY AFRICAN CHURCH

'Religion is the sign of the oppressed creature, the feeling of a heartless world, and the soul of soulless circumstances. It is the opium of the people.
'The abolition of religion as the illusory happiness of the people is the demand for their real happiness. The demand to give up the illusions about their condition is a demand to give up a condition that requires illusion.'
KARL MARX (1818–1883)

'Religion would then be the universal obsessional neurosis of humanity; like the obsessional neurosis of children . . . if this view is right, it is to be supposed that a turning-away from religion is bound to occur with the fatal inevitability of a process of growth . . .'
SIGMUND FREUD (1856–1939), FOUNDER OF PSYCHOANALYSIS

'If religion has given birth to all that is essential to society, it is because society is the soul of religion.'
EMILE DURKHEIM (1858–1917), FOUNDER OF MODERN SOCIOLOGY

Religion has 'its own independent roots in the hidden depths of the spirit itself'.
RUDOLF OTTO (1869–1937)

Primal religions

Hinduism

Buddhism

China: Confucianism, Buddhism, Taoism

Japan: Shinto, Buddhism, New Religions

Jainism and Parsism

Sikhism

Judaism

Christianity

Islam

Areas of low population

Approximate present-day distribution of
the world's religions In all areas, only the
predominant religion has been shown.

1

PRIMAL RELIGIONS

For the people of the world's small-scale ethnic
societies, there is no distinction between religion
and the rest of life.

*The tribal hill peoples of China follow a primal religion
which includes ancestor veneration, as shown here.*

In Africa, the Americas and Australasia live some 250 million people who belong to the so-called 'primal', 'traditional', 'pre-literate', 'small-scale' or 'tribal' societies. For them 'religion' is almost the same thing as 'culture' or 'world-view' (from the German *weltanschauung*); or, as one African author has put it, 'all of life is religious'.

Religion has been defined as the unique attempt of each society to express the meaning of its existence. Often, people's environment is hostile: cyclones blow, thunderstorms rage and volcanoes erupt; nations go to war; and famine and disease, poverty and oppression disturb the balance of living. So their religion provides people with a framework within which to come to terms with their environment and to give their experience meaning.

Primal religions are the religions of small-scale pre-literate societies. They have no religious writings or scriptures. Instead, beliefs are handed down by word of mouth from one generation to another.

Small-scale societies include the islanders of Papua New Guinea and Indonesia, the tribal hill peoples of India, China and South-east Asia, the remaining pockets of American Indians in North America, the Eskimos of Canada, Greenland and Siberia, the Indians of the river valleys, forests and plateaux of South and Central America and, above all, more than 800 ethnic groups on the African continent.

Many of these societies have resisted for centuries the advancing world religions of Hinduism, Buddhism, Judaism, Christianity and Islam. Others have accepted the new religions at one level and at another, deeper level, have persisted in the ways of their predecessors. This has led to mixed religions (syncretism), such as the Christianity of Mexico, the Hinduism of Bali, the Islam of Malaysia, the spirit-possession of South America and the Caribbean, some of the independent and spirit churches of Africa, and the cargo cults of Melanesia.

Rituals

For most people in small-scale societies, especially in Africa, life is punctuated by a series of rituals. Each stage of life, every 'life-crisis', has its rite: birth, puberty, marriage, death. Afflictions, too—from illness, infertility and misfortune to untimely death—are marked by their own rituals. Almost every evening the measured beat of the drum can be heard in the distance, accompanied by singing and dancing, as some rite gets under way.

Initiation

For Kiplagat, a youth of the Nandi people in the highlands of western Kenya, the supremely important moment in life is the moment of circumcision. With the flick of a knife at the climax of a long ritual process, his boyhood becomes a thing of the past and he enters

An African prayer

O God, you are great,
you are the one who created me,
I have no other.
God, you are in the heavens.
You are the only One:
Now my child is sick,
And you will grant me my desire.

manhood. The ritual is a legacy from the past when the Nandi were a warrior people and every young man went through a period of warriorhood.

Although today most Nandi have accepted some form of Christianity, they continue to a large extent to undergo traditional initiation rites supervised by tribal elders. Through their symbolism these rituals reinforce the traditional world-view, and also the identity both of the individual and of the community in the face of a rapidly changing world.

Key people

Medicine men Also called 'herbalists' or 'traditional doctors' (misnamed 'witch-doctors' by outsiders); purveyors of herbal remedies, formally or informally trained, and respected by the community.

Mediums Their task is to communicate with the spirits and the living dead (ancestors).

Diviners Concerned with divination, using mediums, oracles, possession and divination objects such as collections of oddly-shaped bones and roots, gourds, cowrie shells and pebbles; they often employ 'good magic' to counter witchcraft and sorcery.

Shamans They may be prophets or seers in some societies. They exercise control over the spirits.

Ritual experts Rainmakers, circumcision elders, and the like, who perform special duties.

Priests They are set aside for divine service and represent humans to God and God to humans. Strictly, priests are associated with temples and shrines, but in African situations the word also applies to those who perform religious duties in sacred groves and elsewhere.

Witches and sorcerers They employ evil magic against people. Witches use their innate and often involuntary possession of 'witchcraft' and sorcerers use a variety of devices.

Affliction

For Metson, a depressed housewife in the fishing village of Tawang in Kelantan, Malaysia, a significant event is taking place. She is in trance and her 'possessing spirit' is being interrogated by a Malay *shaman*. Her malady is sickness or loss of soul, believed to be caused by malevolent spirits entering and upsetting the delicate 'humoral balance' of her body.

The aim of the seance is to exorcise the spirit, and so to restore her soul. To achieve this, the shaman has to go into trance and through his 'familiar spirit' to interrogate Metson's spirit. Then, once he has determined the nature of the spirit and the cause of possession, he must send it back to its home.

Metson will not remain passive. She must actively desire the departure of the spirit. When the shaman has sent her into trance the spirit can come out into the open and be effectively admonished. In this way there is a public demonstration of the cause of illness and a public treatment. The following evening Metson will take part in a comedy to mark the successful expulsion of the spirit.

Metson lives in an Islamic society in which women have little religious or social status and divorce is often imminent. The seance gives much-needed psychotherapy, especially in cases of illness caused by social stress. It provides a theatre in which she can act out her emotions and come to terms with her role in society.

The first Europeans to observe the Australian Aborigines thought they had no religion. In fact, spiritual beliefs are basic to daily and social relationships for the Aboriginal people. Here a ceremony is enacted to mark the transition from death to spiritual existence.

Beliefs

The religious beliefs of small-scale societies are obviously very varied. Much depends on the environment. But though details differ from group to group, there are certain aspects which recur worldwide, in particular belief in the closeness of spirits and in the living dead. Looking at a number of African tribes will give an idea of how these beliefs work out.

In Ankole, Uganda, the Nkore people believe in Ruhanga the Creator who made all things at once. Ruhanga is personal yet distant. He is the principle of order and is therefore good, but he is reluctant to intervene directly in the affairs of humans. This belief recurs in African religions as the following myth from West Africa shows.

'There was once a woman who had a very long pestle, and when she pounded her corn the wooden pole hit against God who lived just above the sky. One day she gave a great bang, hitting God in the eye, and in anger he went away into the distance, never to return.'

The 'lineage spirits' and the spirits of the living dead are much closer to the Nkore than Ruhanga. The guardian spirits of each tribal lineage group are said to be descended from a legendary ruling dynasty and ultimately from Ruhanga himself.

At least one member of each lineage group must be specially initiated to become, in effect, the priest of the group, responsible for making offerings and for initiating future members into the cult of the lineage spirits. One of the most important results of the cult is that it enables members of the lineage group to co-operate in ensuring successful seedtime and harvest. Otherwise it attracts little attention unless the lineage spirits cause trouble.

It is the spirits of the living dead, the ancestors, who need and receive more attention. They are likely to be malevolent, punishing bad actions and not rewarding good

In all cultures the transition from life to death has been surrounded by ritual. Amongst the Torajo people of Indonesia the funeral of someone from a high-ranking family is likely to last three weeks. The burial place itself contains life-sized wooden models of the dead.

Key concepts

Magic Worldwide, magic denots the attempt to control the course of nature by special powers or actions. It is found in all types of culture, even to some extent in modern scientific society.

Mana The Pacific term for what is known in Africa as 'dynamism', or 'vital force'. It springs from the belief that power (or powers) cn be tapped for the benefit of humanity.

Totem Any object towards which members of a group have a special mystical relationship. It may be an animal, a place, or something inanimate. Totem animals cannot be killed or eaten except under very special circumstances.

Taboo This term applies to any person or thing which is regarded as 'holy' or forbidden and not to be touched.

ones. So care must be taken in the burial of relatives and even of strangers within the household. Neglect brings revenge. As among many peoples, the living dead become the custodians of the moral order.

In other East African societies, such as the Maasai and Nandi, attention is focused on the Supreme Being rather than on the spirits. Among these peoples, God is seen to be more involved, and so he is invoked, often daily, for protection. He is the beneficent creator, the sustainer of life, the arbiter of justice. In other West African societies the Supreme Being is often attended by a host of divinities as well as spirits of people and nature.

2

HINDUISM

Hindus follow the 'eternal religion', an all-embracing way of life and culture which leads them through the cycles of life, death and rebirth.

Hindus cremate their dead and scatter the ashes into the River Ganges—these sacred waters are a symbol of life without end.

The world 'Hindu' is derived from the Persian word for 'Indian', and 'Hinduism' is the religion of the peoples of India. Precise definition, however, is not so simple. Hinduism is a vast subject and an elusive concept. It has no founder and no creed. But it does possess scriptures, and the most ancient of these, the *Rig Veda*, provides a key to understanding Hinduism as a whole.

Some time between the years 1500 and 1200 BC—roughly speaking when Moses was leading the Israelites out of Egypt—wild, charioteering Aryan tribes invaded India from the north-west and settled in what is today the Punjab. They had an important class of priests who composed hymns to their gods for use at sacrifices. Over the years these hymns were committed to memory and remarkably preserved until in later centuries 1,028 of them were enshrined in writing in the *Rig Veda*, the world's oldest living religious literature and Hinduism's most sacred book.

The religion develops

However, as Aryan religion spread, it absorbed elements from the cultures already present, for example from the Indus Valley in the north and the Dravidian in the south. So Hinduism as we know it today is like a great, deep river into which, over a period of more than 3,000 years, many streams have

Scriptures

The Vedas
The *Rig Veda* consists of hymns completed by about 900 BC.
The *Sama Veda* consists of verses mainly taken from the *Rig Veda* and rearranged for chanting at sacrifices.
The *Yajur Veda* is written in prose and gives instructions for those officiating at sacrifices.
The *Atharva Veda* contains magical formulae, written in verse, to help cure disease and bring success in war.

The *Brahmanas* are supplements to the Vedas, containing elaborate explanations of the sacrificial rituals.
The *Upanishads*, dating from about 600 BC, are based on the Vedas but reflect a movement away from rituals to philosophy, particularly the doctrine of reincarnation.

The Law Codes These attempt to regulate Hindu society.

The Great Epics The *Mahabharata* and the *Ramayana* portray in epic stories all the complexity of Hindu belief and practice. The *Mahabharata* contains the best-known and best-loved scripture of modern Hinduism, the *Bhagavad Gita*.

The Puranas These develop the mythology of classical Hinduism in a series of lengthy versified texts from the medieval period.

Key concepts

Brahman The all-pervading, self-existent power, the cosmic unity.

Atman The essence or principle of life: reality in its individual forms, as distinct from *brahman*.

Maya Literally 'illusion'; this world is neither real nor unreal.

Advaita Only one reality exists. All things are one. A strict form of this belief called 'monism' was taught by the Vedanta philosopher, Shankara.

Dharma Moral and religious duty.

Karma Literally 'action'; the inexorable moral law of cause and effect governing the future: bad actions lead to rebirth in the lower orders, perhaps as an animal; good actions lead to rebirth in the higher orders, perhaps as a priest.

Samsara The bondage of life, death and rebirth, governed by the law of *karma*.

Moksha Literally 'release'; liberation from the continuous round of rebirths.

Bhakti Devotion or worship offered to a single deity. Liberation by faith as distinct from liberation by works or knowledge.

current providing unity is the religion which grew out of the *Rig Veda* and later Vedic scriptures. This means that Indian religion has certain discernible features. One of these is the doctrine of reincarnation: the belief that at death the soul always passes into another body until released from the continuous wheel of rebirth.

The many ways of salvation

Hindus number about 700 million. They are mostly to be found in India, but also in other parts of

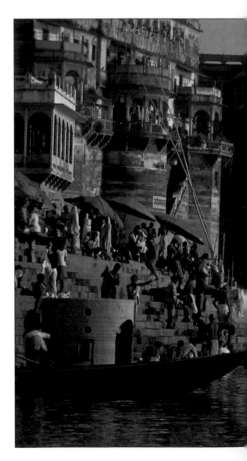

flowed. The streams are the beliefs and practices of the numerous races, ethnic groups and cultures of the Indian subcontinent. This means that there are almost as many versions of Hinduism as there are villages or groups of Hindus.

The underlying and dominant

Asia, Africa, the West Indies and more recently to some degree in Europe and the West. Hinduism offers, broadly speaking, three ways of salvation from the wheel of rebirth. These are: philosophy or knowledge, works of religious observance, and devotion.

So, existing side by side in Hinduism, we find the heights of philosophical reasoning concerning Ultimate Reality, the most patient discipline of concentrated meditation or religious observance, and the dedicated devotion of image-worship associated with countless popular gods. Since the early nineteenth century various reform movements have also arisen as Indians have come into contact with Western culture.

Yet, essentially, to be a Hindu today is to believe in the Hindu way of life and to follow it to the best of one's ability.

Beliefs

Hindus are monotheists at heart; they believe in one High God— Brahman, 'the Absolute'—who rules over the world with the aid of

Hindu pilgrims come to the Ganges to achieve purification through ritual bathing.

The Hindu Gods

The gods of the Vedic period

Agni
The life-force of nature. The god of fire and sacrifice.

Indra
The sky-god and god of war.

Varuna
The upholder of the cosmic order, with power to punish and reward.

The later gods

Brahma—the Creator
The lord of all creatures. He is above and beyond worship, and there are hardly any temples dedicated to him.

Vishnu—the Preserver
The controller of human fate. He draws near to humankind in ten incarnations (avatars). He is generally kindly.

Shiva—the Destroyer
The source of both good and evil. The destroyer of life and also the one who re-creates new life.

Sarasvati
Consort of Brahma. The goddess of knowledge, learning and truth.

Lakshmi
Wife of Vishnu. The goddess of fortune and beauty.

Kali/Durga
Consort of Shiva. The 'great mother'. She is the symbol of judgment and death.

The ten avatars of Vishnu

1 Matsya
The fish. He appeared at the time of the great flood, to warn humanity.

2 Kurma
The tortoise. He rescued treasures from the flood.

3 Varaha
The boar. He raised the earth from the flood.

4 Nara-Simha
The man-lion. He defeated evil demons.

5 Vamana
The dwarf. He defeated evil demons.

6 Parasha-Rama
'Rama with an axe'. He destroyed the members of the Kshatriya warrior caste who threatened to dominate the world.

7 Rama-Chandra
The hero of the Ramayana epic. He was a noble hero who combatted the evil in the world. He is the epitome of virtue.

8 Krishna
As well as being an avatar of Vishnu, Krishna is a god in his own right, the most popular of all the gods. He is also the hero of many myths, depicted as a lover, a warrior and a king.

9 Buddha
'The enlightened one'. The ninth avatar is Gautama, the Buddha founder of Buddhism.

10 Kalki
The tenth avatar is yet to come.

many lesser gods. To the educated Hindu the lesser gods have a status similar to that of saints and angels in certain branches of Christianity. To the ordinary believer or 'village Hindu', however, they are considerably more important.

The religion of these people—popular Hinduism—may be divided into three branches or sects, each with its own view of the nature and name of the High God: Vishnu, Shiva or Shakti. Families, by long tradition, support one branch or another. All branches are to be found in every part of India, though Shaivism is particularly strong in Kashmir in the north and Tamil in the south, and Shaktism in Bengal and Assam. The three sects continue together more or less in harmony, with devotees of one god occasionally worshipping at the shrine of another. Educated Hindus believe that the three gods are merely differing ways of looking at the same High God or Ultimate Reality.

The three sects

Vishnu is generally worshipped in the form of one of his ten incarnations. Wholly of goodwill, he sits enthroned in heaven beside his wife, the goddess Lakshmi. But because of his concern for the world he descends from time to time in the form of an incarnation.

Shiva differs in character from Vishnu. He has a dark and grim side to his nature, which seems to be derived from Rudra, the Vedic god of mountain and storm. Shiva

Krishna playing his flute. Krishna is one of the most popular and important incarnations (avatars) of Vishnu.

is often described as lurking in horrible places such as battlefields and cemeteries. In sculpture he is often shown wearing a garland of skulls and surrounded by evil spirits as he dances the grim dance by which he destroys the world. At other times he is seen as the great ascetic, rapt in continuous meditation in the Himalayas. Devotees worship Shiva in the form of an image and also in his emblem, the *linga*, a short, rounded, phallic pillar which represents the creative power of God. Shaivism has its unpleasant sides too. There is animal sacrifice, and some ascetics deliberately inflict pain on themselves. Most devotees, nonetheless, look on their god as loving and gracious.

To her devotees, Shakti, the great Mother Goddess, is the supreme deity. From their point of view the god in his male aspect is not active in the world and does not need worship. His wife Shakti is worshipped instead, in the fierce form of Durga or Kali and in the mild form of Parvati or Uma. In her fierce form Shakti is often depicted as a repulsive hag, bearing an assortment of weapons and trampling on a demon. Even today her worship is often accompanied by animal sacrifice. In the past, human sacrifice to Durga was not unknown. In her mild form Shakti appears as a beautiful young woman. For although she may unleash her fury on sinners she is loving and benevolent to her devotees.

Other major gods are also worshipped, for example Brahma the Creator, Ganesh the elephant-god, Hanuman the monkey-god and Surya the sun-god.

A way of living

Hinduism is a way of life. It is a path of duty to be followed within a divinely ordered society. The basic unit of society is the family. And so an individual's life is marked at every stage by domestic ritual. Birth, initiation, marriage and death—each has its ritual, as well as rites of daily worship and annual festivals. The individual is reminded that he is part of a family. He is also made aware that the family is part of a caste and the caste part of a social class.

There are four great classes: the priests (*brahmins*), the nobles (*kshatriyas*), the merchants and peasants (*vaishyas*), and the manual labourers (*shudras*). There are also

The wedding ceremony has great personal and religious significance for a Hindu.

Quotes from the Scriptures

There was neither non-existence nor existence then; there was neither the realm of space nor the sky which is beyond. What stirred? Where? In whose protection? Was there water, bottomlessly deep?

There was neither death nor immortality then. There was no distinguishing sign of night nor of day. That one breathed, windless, by its own impulse. Other than that there was nothing beyond.

RIG VEDA 10.129.1–2

Whatever you do, or eat, or give, or offer in adoration, let it be an offering to me; and whatever you suffer, suffer it for me.

Thus thou shalt be free from the bonds of Karma which yield fruits that are evil and good; and with thy soul one in renunciation thou shalt be free and come to me.

I am the same to all beings, and my love is ever the same; but those who worship me with devotion, they are in me and I in them.

For even if the greatest sinner worships me with all his soul, he must be considered righteous, because of his righteous will.

And he shall soon become pure and reach everlasting peace. For this is my word of promise, that he who loves me shall not perish.

For all those who come to me for shelter, however weak or humble or sinful they may be—women or Vaishyas or Shudras—they all reach the Path supreme.

How much more the holy Brahmins and the royal saints who love me! Having come to this world of sorrow, which is transient, love thou me.

Give me thy mind and give me thy heart, give me thy offerings and thy adoration; and thus with thy soul in harmony, and making me thy goal supreme, thou shalt in truth come to me.

KRISHNA TO ARJUNA IN
BHAGAVAD GITA 9.27–34

outcastes and unclassified peoples. All are divided into several castes or sub-classes, each with its appropriate duty. Traditionally, the four classes were looked on as totally separate species. A member of one class would not marry a member of another class—nor even eat a meal with him. Nowadays, however, at least theoretically, such distinctions have been abolished.

A man of the upper three classes, goes through four stages in his life.

There is the stage of the celibate student, the householder, the hermit, and the homeless religious beggar. The first stage is entered at the time of initiation. From then on the man will wear the sacred thread which passes over his left shoulder and under his right arm. Marriage is important, and the wedding ceremony one of the most solemn and complicated rites in Hinduism, because it ensures not only the continuity of the family but also the

Festivals

All kinds of festivals abound in India.

Temple Festivals At least once a year the temple image is taken in public procession with much elaborate festivity.

The Holi Festival Held at the beginning of spring, in February/March. The festival has its roots in an ancient fertility ritual. The crowds sing songs, carry phallic symbols and delight in squirting each other with coloured water and powder.

The Dasera Festival A popular ten-day event in September/October, held in honour of the goddesss Durga. Its origins go back to Rama's victory over Ravana, as told in the *Ramayana*. Great effigies of Ravana filled with crackers and explosives parade the streets, later to be set alight by Rama's fiery arrows.

The Divali Festival The four-day New Year festival; associated with Rama, spirits of the dead, and Vishnu and his wife Lakshmi, goddess of wealth and prosperity. Oil lamps are lit and houses cleaned to welcome Lakshmi, and fireworks explode to send away evil spirits. Business people especially celebrate Divali, opening new account books with prayers to Lakshmi for success in the New Year.

welfare of its dead members in the other world. Only a son can perform the funeral rites which provide the soul of his dead father with a new spiritual body with which to pass on to the next life.

Hinduism in the home

All the most important Hindu rites are performed in the home, not least worship (*puja*). Hindus worship as individuals and families, not as congregations—except in modern reform sects. Most houses have either a room or a corner in which there is a family shrine. The shrine contains an image or emblem of the deity. It may be the spiral marked stone representing Vishnu or the stone pillar representing Shiva. There are brightly-coloured pictures illustrating Hindu mythology or depicting the exploits of the gods. First the worshipper anoints the god, while reciting texts. Then he sits down in front of it to meditate. Incense or joss sticks are lit and flowers and food are placed in front of the shrine. Worship in the temple follows a similar pattern.

The path of duty is the way to salvation: it obtains the release of the soul from the continuous cycle of life, death and rebirth.

3

BUDDHISM

In some of its many different forms, Buddhism is the religion without a god.

This Tibetan Buddhist wall-painting depicts the everlasting round. The wheel is shot through with suffering; death is never far away. But in the background there remains the figure of the Buddha who leads humankind to timeless freedom beyond.

The three jewels

Buddhism's Three Jewels or *triratna* are the Buddha, the Dharma (his doctrine) and the Sangha (the order of monks).

At every Buddhist shrine and meeting the Three Jewels are invoked three times in the simple formula which, it is believed, Gautama gave to his first missionaries:

To the Buddha for refuge I go,
To the Dharma for refuge I go,
To the Sangha for refuge I go.

The Golden Pagoda of Rangoon is the largest and oldest shrine of its kind in the world. It is the spiritual heart of Burma. Its special sanctity arises from the belief that it enshrines relics not only of Gautama the Buddha, the founder of Buddhism, but also of the three previous Buddhas.

Pilgrims arrive on foot and by bus at the hill over which the pagoda is spread in all its splendour, with its courtyards and many chapels. Giant lions guard the pinnacled gateways to the four main entrances. The worshippers remove their shoes and climb long flights of stone steps to a courtyard above. From stalls beside the steps they buy a variety of religious and secular objects: gold leaf to stick on the pagoda, incense sticks, flowers, paper lanterns, images, prayer beads, bells, dolls, drums, combs, buttons and orangeade. At the top each pilgrim strikes a great bell to call heaven and earth to witness the acts of piety about to be performed.

The layperson and the monk

For lay pilgrims, worship (*puja*) is a way of earning merit, and consists of offering gifts and services to the Three Jewels. Worshippers place a large vase of flowers in front of an image of the Buddha. They join their hands in front of their faces, bow, kneel and prostrate themselves. They chant the liturgy and passages of scripture, perform ritual acts of reverence and burn incense. In an offering of inner worship, they contemplate an image of the Buddha.

Outside the pagoda, at the foot of one of the giant guardian lions, is a young monk, or *bhikku*, chanting the liturgy as he counts the beads of the rosary. For him, as for the pilgrim, worship is individual, not communal. Moreover, acts of worship are in origin performed by monks, not by laypeople. For the

Marks of existence

Dhukka, suffering Birth is suffering, decay is suffering, death is suffering; sorrow, lamentation, pain, grief and despair are suffering.

Anicca, Impermanence All things rise, pass and change; all things are vanishing and dissolving from moment to moment.

Anatta, not-self The idea of a permanent, unchanging ego as the basis of individual personality is a fiction.

Clearly identifiable, with their shaved heads and yellow robes, Buddhist monks devote their lives to prayer and devotion.

monk is Buddhism's norm, perhaps the only true Buddhist. It is said that if a layman gains the Buddhist bliss (*nirvana*) it is because he has been a monk in a previous existence.

The monk is marked out by his yellow or saffron robes—consisting of three garments—his shaven head, and beard. His only possessions are his robe, an alms bowl, a razor, a needle and a water-strainer. He begs for his food. In the Buddhist lands of South-east Asia, every morning monks are to be seen on their begging-round, holding their lacquer-ware alms bowls in outstretched hands.

Monks enter the order (*sangha*) by means of special ordination ceremonies. They are not, however, bound to the monastic life for ever: they may leave whenever they wish. In certain countries, all boys spend some time, perhaps as little as a week, in a monastery, as part of their religious education. Others enter a monastery during the rainy season in order to meditate.

The two Buddhisms

There are two distinct types of Buddhism, Theravada and Mahayana, springing from a common root. Theravada is often called the 'Little Vehicle' and Mahayana the 'Great Vehicle', since the Buddhist doctrine is conceived as a vehicle, a raft or a ship, which carries us across the ocean of the world of suffering to a 'Beyond'—to salvation, to bliss.

Theravada is the earliest form of Buddhism. Its teaching is based on a collection of doctrines, which was approved at an important conference held soon after Gautama's death and offers salvation to the monk alone. Mahayana belongs to the second phase of Buddhist thought. Its crystallization coincides with the beginning of the Christian era, and its teaching opens up the way of salvation to all.

The vast majority of Buddhists adhere to Mahayana and belong overwhelmingly to the northern countries of Nepal, Tibet, Vietnam, China, Korea and Japan. Theravad is dominant in the south-east Asian countries of Sri Lanka, Burma, Thailand, Laos and Kampuchea. In India, land of its birth, Buddhism is a minority religion currently undergoing revival. In China, Tibet, Vietnam, Laos and Kampuchea, Buddhism is under threat and its survival uncertain. And in the West Buddhism is enjoying increasing acceptance. Estimates of the extent of Buddhism vary from 200–400 million.

The roof top of a Buddhist monastery near Lhasa in Tibet. A place of peace for contemplation and a centre of religious instruction for young Buddhist boys.

Gautama the Buddha

According to tradition the founder of Buddhism was Siddhartha Gautama who, most probably, lived from 563 to 483 BC. What is known of his life and teachings is based on the scriptures of Theravada Buddhism. These were written in the ancient Pali language about 400 years after Gautama's death, and until that time had been carried in the memories of successive generations of disciples. For early Buddhism it was the word of its founder, rather than his life, which was of greatest importance. Consequently, there was no full-scale biography until the second

The Noble Eightfold Path

The earliest and most basic description of the Path is that it is threefold. The three parts, morality, meditation and wisdom, are to be pursued simultaneously.

The Path

- Right View
- Right Resolve
- Right Speech
- Right Action
- Right Livelihood
- Right Effort
- Right Concentration
- Right Contemplation or Ecstasy

Morality Expressed in the Five Precepts.

Meditation Liberation, mind control and the cessation of sense experience.

Wisdom Grasping the Four Noble Truths and resolving to observe them.

The four Noble Truths

- The noble truth of suffering. All mortal existence is characterized by suffering.
- The noble truth of the origin of suffering. Suffering arises from craving or desire.
- The noble truth of the cessation of desire. To stop desire means to stop suffering.
- The noble truth of the way to the cessation of desire. The stopping of desire comes by following the Noble Eightfold Path pioneered by the Buddha.

Throughout the Buddhist world, images of Buddha are similar. The largest image is the Daibutsu in Japan which was cast in bronze over 700 years ago.

century AD. However, we may be reasonably certain about the essential facts of his life.

Nepal. Throughout his early life his father sought to protect him from the sorrows of the world. He was reared in delightful palaces, schooled in the princely arts and married to a beautiful princess who bore him a son. However, while his son was still an infant, Gautama began to be disturbed by the problem of suffering. Despite his father's efforts, he eventually escaped his sheltered environment. Outside he met, one after the other, an old man in the last stages of senility, a sick man afflicted by disease, a corpse being carried to the cremation ground and, finally, a shaven-headed, wandering religious beggar, clad in a simple yellow robe, but radiating peace and joy.

Renunciation and enlightenment

Then came the *great renunciation*. Gautama resolved to leave his wife and infant son and to live the life of an ascetic. For six years, with five companions, he strove to find release from the weariness of existence. By the end he was reduced to skin and bones; yet he had not attained his goal. He therefore left his companions and went to meditate under a Bo-tree by the River Gaya. It was there that he received the *great enlightenment*. He discerned that suffering and its cause, desire, were at the root of the troubles of humankind. Moreover, desire could be stopped by following the Middle Way between the extremes of sensuousness and asceticism.

Gautama then went to the deer park at Benares. There he preached his first sermon to his five former companions, so as to 'set in order the Wheel of Dharma'. The five became his first disciples (*arhats*) and were joined a few days later by a band of sixty others. Thus was founded the nucleus of the Buddhist order of monks. For eight months of the year they would travel from place to place preaching, and then for the four months of the rainy season they would live in bamboo huts in great parks donated by wealthy lay followers—a basis for the great monasteries of later years.

Gautama died at the age of 80.

Scriptures

The teachings of Buddhism are found in collections of scriptures called the 'three baskets' or *Tripitaka* and also in the scriptures of the different schools of Buddhism.

The Tripitaka

The *Vinaya Pitaka* deals with monastic discipline. The *Sutra* (or *Dharma*) Pitaka deals with doctrine, for example the Buddha story, theories of the self and rebirth, the Three Jewels and the Precepts. The *Abhidharma Pitaka* deals with advanced doctrine and philosophy.

The Dhammapada or 'path of Nature' is the oldest Buddhist text. It is quite short but of great importance and contains the Four Noble Truths, the Noble Eightfold Path and many teachings on practical morality and self-discipline.

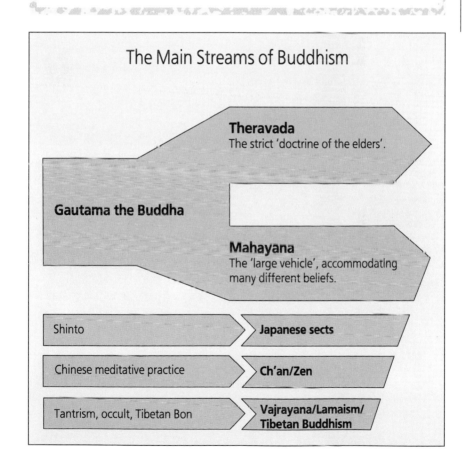

The Main Streams of Buddhism

Gautama the Buddha

Theravada
The strict 'doctrine of the elders'.

Mahayana
The 'large vehicle', accommodating many different beliefs.

Shinto → **Japanese sects**

Chinese meditative practice → **Ch'an/Zen**

Tantrism, occult, Tibetan Bon → **Vajrayana/Lamaism/Tibetan Buddhism**

While the Buddha himself is unique in history, other human beings are called to become Buddhas, though according to the oldest teaching only a few will reach this goal.

Quotes from the Scriptures

If you see the evil others do, and if you feel you disapprove, be careful not to do likewise, for people's deeds remain with them.

Those who cheat in business deals, those who act against the Dharma, those who swindle, those who trick—not only harm their fellow-men, they hurl themselves into a gorge, for people's deeds remain with them.

Whatever deeds a man may do, be they delightful, be they bad, they make a heritage for him; deeds do not vanish without trace.

A man will steal while profit seems to lie that way. Then others steal from him, and so the thief by thieving is undone.

The fool, while sinning, thinks and hopes, 'This never will catch up with me.' Wait till you're in the other world, and there the fate of sinners learn.

DHAMMAPADA 4A

His body was cremated by his disciples and the ashes divided between eight clan groups. Each built an elaborate sacred cairn or *stupa* to house the relic. For lay Buddhists these *stupas* became the focus of devotion and were later developed into the pagodas.

The way to release

Buddhism's Middle Way appears to be a religion of self-effort without reference to the gods. Yet this statement needs to be qualified, because the idea of the self in Buddhism is distinctive. The self or soul is made up of five elements or *skandhas*—body, feelings, perception, impulses and consciousness—and it is constantly changing. It is not a 'permanent self' which connects a person's new life to the life of his or her former existence. Rather it is the 'deeds' of *karma* (the inexorable law of cause and effect) which link one existence to another. The goal of human existence is *nirvana*, and *karma* is no more. *Nirvana* is not annihilation, not nothingness, and yet it is formless and uncreated.

It was inevitable that later Buddhism should develop a doctrine of salvation attainable by all people, not just by the monks. It is a doctrine of salvation by faith and not by works and is exemplified in the Buddhism of China and Japan.

The Precepts

Regularly, in their devotions, monks and lay people undertake to refrain from five things:

- Causing injury to living things
- Taking that which is not given
- Sexual immorality
- Falsehood
- The use of alcohol and drugs since they tend to cloud the mind.

Some lay people follow a more advanced degree and, especially on holy days, undertake with the monks to abstain from:

- Taking food after midday
- Dancing, singing and amusements
- The use of garlands, cosmetics and personal adornments.

Monks also undertake to refrain from:

- Accepting gold and silver
- The use of a luxurious bed.

4

CHINA

Today, after thirty years of suppression, religion is once more coming to life in China.

The traditional three 'ways' of religion in China—Confucianism, Taoism and Buddhism—have re-emerged and intertwined with folk religion to form a vital part of life in China today.

China is the land of the three 'ways': Confucianism, Taoism and Buddhism. In their origins, the three are distinct. Confucianism gave new impetus to the ancient practice of ancestor worship, Taoism provded a mystical interpretation of the world and Mahayana Buddhism brought the possibility of salvation to all by grace through faith and devotion. But in their development, all three have intertwined or even merged with each other and with the folk religion which centred on home and farm.

In recent centuries, world religions such as Christianity and Islam have also exercised some influence. And, more recently still, Marxism has displayed all the influence and appeal of a fourth religion. Yet what the future holds is unknown. Since the republican revolution of 1911 the State rites have disappeared and ancestor veneration has dwindled. Since the communist revolution of 1949 Confucianism has been condemned as impeding progress and social change, Taoism has been controlled and Buddhism tolerated. Yet Confucius' tomb was restored in 1962, the temples of Beijing have been beautified and reopened to the public and at least 50 million people profess to be conscientious devotees of the Buddha.

Confucianism

The founder of Confucianism, K'ung-fu-tzu, or Confucius as Christian missionaries called him, was born in 551 BC in the city-state of Lu in northern China, and died in 479 BC. Although later legend made him of aristocratic descent, he himself is reputed to have said: 'When young I was without rank and in humble circumstances.' He was to become one of the world's most famous teachers.

His times were fraught with chaos and uncertainty and the administration of China was taken over by experts in writing and ritual called *Ju*. It is thought that Confucius was one of these; but he failed to secure a place in administration and so took up teaching. He gathered round him a group of students to discuss the

---

Confucian Scriptures

Six Chinese classics

- The Book of History (*Shu Ching*)
- The Book of Poetry (*Shi Ching*)
- The Book of Changes (*I Ching*)
- The Book of Rites (*Li Chi*)
- The Book of Music (*Yueh Ching*)
- Spring and Autumn Annals (*Ch'un Chu'u*)

Four books

- The Analects (*Lun Yu*)
- The Great Learning (*Ta Hsueh*)
- The Doctrine of the Mean (*Chung Yung*)
- The Book of Mencius (*Meng Tzu Shu*)

Key concepts in Confucianism

Li Literally 'rites', but for Confucius it came to mean 'good manners', propriety, the code of gentlemanly conduct.

Jen Goodness or virtue in the sense of unselfishness, deference towards others, courtesy and loyalty to family and prince.

Hsaio Filial piety, from which developed the *five relationships*:

- between father and son;
- between elder and younger brothers;
- between husband and wife;
- between elder and younger;
- between ruler and subject.

Chan-tzu The superior person, the virtuous, the gentleman.

T'ien Heaven, that which inspired Confucius. Most likely it included a supreme providential Being.

Tao The way, the pursuit of virtue and harmony in social living.

Shu The principle of 'reciprocity'. It is summed up in Confucius' negative expression of the Golden Rule: 'What you do not want done to yourself, do not do to others.'

moral, social and political problems of the day. He taught more by debate than by systematic lecturing and his teaching in its most original form is to be found in *The Analects*, a collection of discussions and sayings.

Confucius taught the importance of *li*, which means propriety or orderliness. And the Confucian ideal of the 'gentleman' whose life is governed by propriety gradually emerged. The gentleman is serious in personal conduct, respectful to superiors, just and kindly disposed to the people. He is also concerned with 'filial piety', his duty as a son

A ceremony at a Confucian temple. Although Confucianism is best known for its moral philosophy, it also emphasizes worship, ritual and sacrifice.

Key concepts in Taoism

Tao The way. This is threefold in meaning: it is the Ultimate Reality; the Principle controlling the universe; and the way of living in harmony with the universe.

Te Virtue, power, the psychic magnetism of the human personality.

Wu wei Actionless activity, passivity. The basis of the Taoist ethic is

for human beings to imitate the effortlessness of nature.

Laissez-faire government Actionless activity applied to the political sphere. This implies a form of anarchy: 'ruling by not ruling'.

Yin and yang The ancient principle of activity and passivity.

Yang denotes the active masculine energy and *yin* the passive feminine one; heaven is active and earth passive. Taoism is *yin*-like. Good is often identified with the *yang* and bad with the *yin*.

to care for his parents, and he venerates the ancestors. This emphasis on filial piety led to the association of Confucius' name with the ancestral cults, although of course they had existed before his time.

As so often happens, Confucius' students experienced greater success than their master. It was his successors Meng Tzu (Mencius, about 390–350 BC) and Hsun Tzu (about 312–238 BC) who spread his fame and enlarged his ideas.

Many Confucians believe Confucianism to be a way of life, a code of moral and social behaviour, rather than a religion. Thus they need not believe in any god. Alternatively they may follow their master, Confucius, and at the same time profess another religion.

The Way

The word *Tao* means literally a path or a way. It may denote a way of acting or a principle of teaching. Confucianism emphasizes the former and Taoism the latter. Tao is the inexpressible Source of all being, the First Cause, the Ultimate Reality. It is the Principle which moderates and controls the universe, the Way in which people live in harmony with the universe.

The original teachings of Taoism are to be found in China's most influential book, the *Tao Te Ching*. The book is attributed to Lao Tzu (born 604 BC), but is now believed to be an anthology of brief passages dating from about the fourth century BC. Lao Tzu's very

existence is disputed today: his name means 'Old Master', a title applied to a number of teachers in the period following Confucius.

To follow the Tao is to follow the way of nature, the 'watercourse way'. Water flows softly and effortlessly to humble places; yet even so it can be the most overpowering of substances. So, too, with the followers of *philosophical Taoism*. They are likely to be mystical and quietist: by stilling the self, their senses and appetites, they can gain an inner perception of the Tao, a oneness with the Eternal, a harmony with

Taoism turns away from society to the contemplation of nature. Taoist monasteries, like this one in China, are centres of mysticism, meditation and ritual prayer.

The ornate doors to a Taoist temple. Temples are attended by priests, and worshippers visit them to seek cures for illness and power over death.

the Principle underlying and penetrating the whole world. They attain a kind of enlightenment not unlike Buddhists engaged in yoga.

Te means virtue or power, and followers of *popular Taoism* seek to harness this power through magic and ritual. They are likely to be preoccupied with death and the quest for immortality.

A Taoist funeral in China. Close relatives dressed in shrouds burn symbolic paper money.

41

A Taoist Scripture

The Way that can be taken is not the
eternal Way,
and the name which can be named
is not the eternal name.
From the nameless come heaven
and earth;
the named is the mother of the
myriad things.
Eternally without desire the one can
see the mystery;
Eternally with desire, that sees the
manifested world.
The two come from the same
source, but their names differ:
Darkness within darkness, the
gateway to all mystery.
The myriad things of the world wax
And return then to the source
As one watches them.
Quietness: that is the name of the
return to the source.
Fulfilling that is eternal nature.
Knowing the eternal is
enlightenment;
But not knowing the eternal brings
disaster.

OPENING LINES OF THE *TAO TE CHING*

The New Buddhism

Mahayana Buddhism penetrated
China from outside around the first
century BC. At first, it met with
resistance. Its doctrine of rebirth
and emphasis on the monastic life
appeared to conflict with Chinese
respect for the ancestors and the
importance of the family. But later
it was to make great progress
because of its liberal doctrines.

In the most important of
Mahayana scriptures, the *Lotus
Sutra*, Sakyamuni, the glorified
Buddha, declares a new revelation:
salvation is by faith. All are called
to bliss. All will one day become
Buddhas.

This new teaching included
countless Buddhas. Maitreya, the
Buddha-to-come, or laughing
Buddha, is a popular figure, for he
will bring happiness and good
fortune. So too is Amitabha who
presides over the Pure Land or
Western Paradise beyond the west
China mountains. Devotees pray to
Maitreya for wealth and to
Amitabha for guidance in the ship
of salvation over the sea of sorrows
to Paradise. The Bodhisattvas are
also important. They are the
enlightened beings who have
denied themselves *nirvana* out of
compassion for struggling
humanity.

One reason why Buddhism was
accepted was its common ground
with Taoism—quiet and
meditation. The special Chinese
brand of Buddhist meditation called
Ch'an is better known to the
modern world by its Japanese
name, Zen.

5

JAPAN

Once the tool of the powerful emperor, religion in Japan now has a new vitality.

Japan presents us with a mingling of religious traditions. Its ancient religions are still followed despite the apparently secular nature of modern industrial Japan.

Festivals are important to Shintoism. Much of Shinto practice is an individual matter, but the festivals which take place at particular shrines bring worshippers together. This temple dancer at the Fushimi Inari shrine is celebrating the popular New Year festival.

On the surface it would appear that the people of modern, industrialized Japan take little interest in religion. But to judge by the great number of religious groups and the multitudes of worshippers seen entering temples and shrines, particularly on such occasions as New Year, this first impression is false. The religiosity of the Japanese is confirmed by recent censuses which show that the majority of Japanese people still claim to have some kind of religious affiliation. Such multiplicity and complexity is undoubtedly related to the tendency of Japanese culture to borrow and assimilate.

Japan, like China, presents us with a mingling of religious traditions. The three most important are Shinto, Buddhism and Confucianism. Shinto has been Japan's own religion for over 2,000 years. Buddhism and Confucianism

The Gion festival (shown here) which takes place in Kyoto is one of Japan's most famous festivals.

Worshippers at a Shinto shrine purify themselves, then approach the shrine and ring a bell or knock to attract the attention of the kami.

Shinto writings

Shinto has no collection of Scripture. It has instead a mythology recorded in two texts from the early eighth century AD (*Kojiki* and *Nihongi*) and a manual of ritual prayers (*Engishiki*) dating from AD 927.

According to Shinto mythology, the age of the Kami began when the cosmos emerged out of chaos. The most important Kami was the Sun Kami, Amaterasu-O-mikami. The age of human history began when Ninigi, grandchild of the Sun Kami descended to the lower regions and his great-grandson, Jimmu Tenno, became the first emperor of a unified Japan.

have both profoundly influenced the spiritual and social life of the Japanese people since the sixth century AD. Christianity has been an important cultural and intellectual influence since its introduction first in the sixteenth century and again in the nineteenth. In addition to these there are the New Religions, which have developed during transitional and unstable periods, and the Folk Religion which can be seen in the syncretistic beliefs of the ordinary people.

Shinto

Shinto is not a Japanese word. It was coined from the Chinese *shen* (gods) and *tao* (way) when Buddhism first entered Japan. The intention was to distinguish the older religion, 'the Way of the Kami' from the new Buddhism. Kami is a

difficult word to translate. It is applied to animals, birds and plants; seas and mountains; all natural phenomena; and even to the ancestors. It expresses a feeling of awe and wonder, a sense of the 'numinous'. According to popular belief there are 8 million Kami.

Ancient Shinto combined this veneration of nature with rites of an early agricultural fertility cult. Traces of both can be seen today in worship of one of the foremost Kami, the Sun Goddess Amaterasu, at the famous shrine of Ise; at pilgrimage to the summit of the holy Mount Fuji; in planting and harvesting ceremonies; and in the veneration of sacred trees.

Sects of Japanese Buddhism

Tendal Introduced by Dengyo (AD 767–822). It stresses one ultimate reality and teaches that salvation comes through meditation and faith.

Shingon This sect drew on many sources. It was introduced by Kobo (AD 774–835), and affirms that at the heart of the universe lies mystery, which is expressed through symbol and ritual.

Jodo Begun by Honen (AD 1133–1212). It stresses faith in Amida (Amitabha) Buddha and teaches that salvation for all can be given from outside; repetition of Amida's name leads to birth into the Pure Land.

Jodo Shinshu Founded by Shinran (AD 1173–1262), one of Honen's favourite disciples. With its emphasis on faith as complete passivity it appeals to lay people.

Zen Flourished with Eisai (AD 1141–1215). It teaches that enlightenment comes from within, through meditation.

Nichiren Founded by Nichiren (AD 1222–82). It emphasizes devotion to the Buddha, doctrine and scripture, and is marked by nationalist emphasis, syncretistic tendencies, and the emergence of lay Buddhism.

Sect Shinto

The thirteen branches of Sect Shinto divide into five groups.

Pure Shinto This emphasizes loyalty to the throne and veneration of the ancestors.

Confucian Sects A combination of Confucianism and Shinto.

Mountain Sects Groups which believe their gods live in sacred mountains.

Purification Sects They insist on physical and ritual purity.

Faith-healing Sects These include the groups founded by Bunjiro (who taught belief in one God and the universal love and brotherhood of all) and Maekawa Miki (who taught the spiritual nature of sickness and evil, and encouraged purification rituals as a cure). Together they claim 7 million members.

Buddhism in Japan

Mahayana Buddhism came to Japan by way of Korea. Between AD 550 and 600, various Korean princes sent gifts of images, scriptures and missionaries to the Japanese imperial court. The princes assured the emperors that Buddhism was a charm to ensure national welfare. For some time its fortunes varied, until a pro-Buddhist clan won control of the imperial house. First, under the devout and statesmanlike regent Shotoku, and later, for a period of more than 1,000 years, Japan honoured Mahayana Buddhism as the state religion. Buddhist priests took over Shinto shrines and re-interpreted Shinto beliefs according to Buddhist doctrine. However, because of Buddhism's characteristic tolerance, Shinto rites underwent few changes and Shinto shrines were carefully preserved. This is often called *Dual Shinto*.

Religion and nationalism

For many centuries, Buddhism dominated Japan. But its supremacy was to end. From the fifteenth century onwards, influences for change came from both inside and outside Japan.

But it was the opening up of Japan to western influence in the eighteenth and nineteenth centuries which proved decisive. Japan's heritage was recovered and restored to its former glory. Pure Shinto was revived. Its spokesmen were interested above all in instilling love of country, reverence for the emperor, filial piety and loyalty to the government. They wanted to reinforce the nationalist concept of a strong centralized State. And so in 1890 an imperial edict declared that *State Shinto*,

despite its use of Shinto mythology and religious ceremony, was non-religious. All Japanese citizens must follow it. Christians and others objected to this infringement of religious freedom, but they were assured that the compulsory rites of State Shinto had no significance except as patriotic exercises.

The whole enterprise came to a sorry end when, after defeat in World War II, the emperor was forced to denounce '... the fictitious ideas that the emperor is manifest god and that the Japanese people are a race superior to other races and therefore destined to rule the world.'

Religious revival

The state monopoly of religion had left people cold. Now there was a popular demand for some warmth and vitality in religion and this led to the development of *Sect Shinto*. In 1882, religious organizations had been divided into three categories:

A Zen temple rock garden, designed to aid meditation.

The traditional tea ceremony features in Zen Buddhism as a means of withdrawl from the everyday world.

Buddhist, Christian and Shinto. Those that could not be classified as Buddhist or Christian were classified as Shinto sects. Thus began the distinction between *Shrine* and *Sect* Shinto. Sect Shinto is characterized by diverse elements such as spirit possession, divination, healing and the practice of magic. Today it has thirteen branches or 'churches', most of which have little in common.

However, nowadays, Shinto sects are commonly known as New Religions, although not all the new religions have a Shinto background. Two of the best known, Tenri-kyo and Konko-kyo, arose in the middle of the last century among the peasants and urban workers. Today they appeal to the middle classes as well. There are said to be well over 100 new religions, varying in size but counting their membership in millions. And new ones are constantly arising, encouraged by the granting of religious freedom after World War II.

Japanese Buddhism, meanwhile, is still influential. Over the centuries it has adapted and assimilated many of the Chinese schools of Buddhism as well as developing its own. The best-known in the West, though by no means the largest, is Zen. Zen was adapted from the Chinese Ch'an, whose method of meditation resembled the self-awareness of Theravada Buddhism. Its aesthetic quality has permeated Japanese life. It has become well known for its adptation of the secular and even the military arts to the pursuit of enlightenment. Examples are its use of archery, flower arrangement, and even motorcycle maintenance! By undergoing the discipline of each art a person is brought to achieve a kind of 'ordered spontaneity'. Zen discipline, together with the Confucian ethic of orderliness, helped to form the ethos of the Japanese warrior class. But, for many, Zen is linked with the calm and orderly ritual of the tea ceremony, or the peace and serenity of the seemingly formless sand-garden.

6

JAINISM

To the Jain, every living thing is sacred.
Cruel actions darken the soul, and the most cruel of
all is to take life.

*Several fine places of temple architecture tell of the ancient glory of the
Jains. This picture is of the magnificent complex at Ranakpur, Rajusthan,
famous for the delicate workmanship in marble.*

For a religion of only 3 million people, almost all of whom live in India, Jainism has wielded an influence out of all proportion to its size and distribution. This influence has been felt most keenly in the modern world through Mahatma Gandhi who, allthough not a Jain, followed its most distinctive doctrine—non-violence to living things, *ahimsa*

The eternal universe

Jains believe that the universe is eternal, without beginning or end. It is uncreated and so there is no Creator. The universe passes through an infinite number of cosmic cycles, each divided into phases of ascent and descent, during which civilization rises and

Five vows of the monk

The life of the Jain monk is strict in the extreme. He vows to renounce five things:

- Killing
- Stealing
- Lying
- Sexual activity
- The possession of property.

falls. At the peak period, men reach an enormous size and a tremendous age. In each cycle, 24 Tirthankaras, or 'fordmakers', appear, to gain liberation for themselves and to guide others across 'the river of transmigration'. The final three

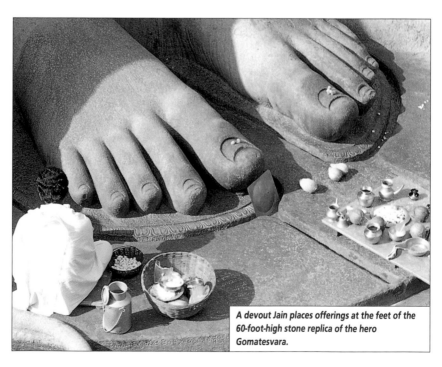

A devout Jain places offerings at the feet of the 60-foot-high stone replica of the hero Gomatesvara.

The perils of existence

The pessimism of Jainism is nowhere better illustrated than in the famous parable of the man in the well, said to have been told by a Jain monk to a prince in order to persuade him of the evils of the world.

There was once a man who, oppressed by his poverty, left home and set out for another country. But after a few days he lost his way and found himself wandering in a dense forest. There, he met a mad elephant which charged him with upraised trunk. Immediately he turned to flee there appeared before him a terrible demoness with a sharp sword in her hand. In fear and trembling he looked about him in all directions for a way of escape until he saw a great tree and ran towards it. But he could not climb its smooth bole and, afraid of death, flung himself into an old well nearby. As he fell he managed to catch hold of a clump of reeds growing from the wall, and clung to them desperately. For below him he could see a mass of writhing snakes, enraged at the sound of his falling, and at the very bottom, identifiable from the hiss of its breath, a mighty black python with its mouth wide open to receive him. And even as he realized that his life could last only as long as the reeds held fast, he looked up and saw two mice, one black and one white, gnawing at the roots. Meanwhile, the elephant, enraged at not catching its victim, charged the tree and dislodged a honeycomb. It fell upon the man clinging so precariously. But even as the bees angrily stung his body, by chance a drop of honey fell on his brow, rolled down his face and reached his lips, to bring a moment's sweetness. And he longed for yet more drops and so forgot the perils of his existence.

Now hear its interpretation. The man is the soul, his wandering in the forest is existence. The wild elephant is death, the demoness old age. The tree is salvation, where there is no fear of death, but which no sensual man can attain. The well is human life, the snakes are passions, and the python hell. The clump of reeds is man's allotted span, the black and white mice the dark and light halves of the month. The bees are diseases and troubles, while the drops of honey are but trivial pleasures. How can a wise man want them, in the midst of such peril and hardship?

51

A layman's salvation

Full salvation is not possible for the layman unless, as the end approaches, he takes the vow of old age, containing the promise to die by voluntary self-starvation. And, according to the Digambaras, it is never possible for a woman unless she is first of all reborn as a man.

Jainism recognizes four sources of *karma*:

- Attachment to things of this life, such as food, clothing, lodging, women and jewels

- Giving rein to anger, pride, deceit and greed

- Uniting the body, mind and speech to worldly things

- False belief.

Karma can be controlled by renouncing all activity. Jainism also recognizes eight kinds of *karma*, three tenses of karma and fourteen steps to liberation from *karma*. Between steps one and four a person acquires knowledge and faith, but only on the fifth step does he realize the importance of conduct and thus become able to take the twelve vows which mark the layman's religious life.

'fordmakers' of the present phase (of rapid decline) are well known in the history of ancient India; the last, Vardhamana Mahavira, died probably in 468 BC. It is from the Sanskrit equivalent to 'fordmakers', *Jinas*, meaning 'conquerors', that Jains derive their name.

Mahavira, the last fordmaker

Mahavira was a contemporary of the Buddha. Like the Buddha, he rejected the religious way of the priests (*brahmins*) for the atheistic way of the possessionless teachers (*shramanas*).

Of noble birth, according to one tradition he was a life-long bachelor; according to another he was married to a princess who bore him a son. Either way, at the age of 28 he plucked out his hair, put on a single garment and set out to live

A Jain man with an umbrella to keep insects away. To injure living things, even unwittingly, is to engender the most harmful of karmic effects. Some Jains wear a cloth across their mouth to prevent them accidentally swallowing insects.

Jain temples do not normally enshrine the images of gods but only of the Tirthankaras. In practice many Jains pray to Hindu gods for help and many Jain temples house images of Hindu deities.

the life of an ascetic. In the thirteenth month he discarded the encumbering garment in favour of nudity, and in the thirteenth year he attained the knowledge of all things—omniscience. Then, for the next 30 years, he taught a great number of followers, monks, nuns and laity alike, the path to 'passionless detachment'. At the age of 72 he starved himself to death. He is regarded as a great teacher and the great example to be followed.

Salvation through non-violence

Jains believe that the individual consists of a soul closely bound up in matter. Salvation is to be found by freeing the soul from matter, so that it may enjoy omniscient self-sufficient bliss for all eternity—the Jain *nirvana*.

The soul is naturally bright and omniscient, but it is liable to get clouded over by *karmic* matter, the result of all action. Selfish, careless or cruel actions darken the soul, but selfless, thoughtful and kind actions can help to lighten it. The most cruel of actions is to take life. And as all living things have souls, including plants and everything derived from the earth, Jains are strongly vegetarian and restricted in their possible work. The most preferred jobs are trading and money-lending and so many Jains have become wealthy merchants and bankers.

7

SIKHISM

In the West, as in their native India, Sikh communities are a vigorous, active influence on society.

The Golden Temple at Amritsar is the central shrine of Sikhism and its most important place of pilgrimage.

Sikhs can be found in almost every part of the world. Their temples adorn the cities of Britain, East Africa, Malaysia, the west coast of Canada, and the United States. The vast majority of Sikhs, however—about 10 million of them—live in India. And of these, about 90 per cent are to be found in the Punjab: 'a tiny island in the sea of Hinduism'. Yet their influence in the life of India greatly exceeds their numerical strength. They are renowned for their progressive farming, their role in the armed forces, sport and the transport industry, and to a lesser extent in manufacturing industry, commerce and the professions.

Guru Nanak

Sikhs trace their origin to Guru Nanak who was born in AD 1469. Nanak spent his childhood in the village of Talvandi, forty miles south-west of Lahore. Before leaving the village he was married and had two sons. But at some point close to the year 1500 he forsook his married life for that of a wandering ascetic. Like a Hindu holy man he wore the saffron robe but like a Muslim he also wore a turban and carried a rosary.

It would be too simplistic to say that Guru Nanak formed a synthesis of these two major religions. But it is true to say that he owed a great deal to a synthesis already in existence, the Sant Tradition of Northern India. This tradition combined elements from the personal devotion of popular

---

Key terms

Amrit The 'nectar of immortality', sugar crystal and water solution used at initiation (*pahul*).

Karah parshad A food made of flour, sugar and ghee in equal proportions, shared at the end of the Sikh gatherings to symbolize casteless equality and brotherhood.

Langar Free kitchen

Mela Fair, festival

Seva Service

Hinduism (*bhakti*), the contemplative experience of mystical Islam (*Sufism*) and the controlled ritual practices of Tibetan Buddhism (*Tantrism*). Nanak expressed the synthesis in a new way, with great beauty and clarity.

Nanak's teaching

It was particularly ideas about salvation which he brought to maturity. The theory held by the Sant tradition was at best incomplete and often naïve. Salvation depended on the single repetition of a particular divine name. Underlying Guru Nanak's new doctrine of salvation were two sets of basic assumptions—concerning the nature of God and the nature of humankind.

God is single and personal, the transcendant Creator with whom the individual must develop the

The ten Gurus

What we in the West call Sikhism, Sikhs call *Gurmat*, 'the Guru's doctrine'. God, the original Guru, imparted his message to his chosen disciple, Nanak, and thereafter to a series of ten gurus:

- Nanak (1469–1539), a strict monotheist, mystic and opponent of asceticism.

- Angad (1504–1552), a consolidator, compiler of hymns and builder of temples.

- Amar Das (1479–1574), the divider of the land, initiator of communal meals. He emphasized the equality of humankind

- Ram Das (1534–1581), a social reformer and founder of Amritsar, the place of worship and pilgrimage

- Arjan (1563–1606), the first guru born a Sikh, builder of the Golden Temple at Amritsar, compiler of hymns and teachings of the Gurus to form the *Adi Granth*.

- Hargobind (1595–1644), the founder of the army which was advised by his father

- Har Rai (1630–1661)

- Har Krishan (1656–1664)

- Tegh Bahadur (1621–1675), brave and generous

- Gobind Singh (1666–1708), the founder of the Khalsa, installer of the Granth as Guru, reviser of the Granth.

most intimate of relationships. Guru Nanak expressed this understanding of God in a number of important terms: God is without form (*nirankar*), eternal (*akal*) and ineffable (*alakh*). Great emphasis is given to the third idea: essentially, God is unknowable. How then can he be known? He can be known because he is a God of grace, concerned that humankind should possess the means of salvation. He therefore reveals himself, in a way that is visible to all who will open their eyes and see. He is 'everywhere present', pervading all creation, particularly the human heart.

But people are wilfully blind. They shut their eyes to this divine revelation which lies within and without. They know that they need salvation but seek it through futile religious exercises, such as worship at Hindu temples or prayers in Muslim mosques. But externals of this kind only bind them even more firmly to the wheel of birth, death and rebirth.

The way to the divine harmony

Guru Nanak's teachings about salvation are expressed in a number of key words which recur throughout his works. They are the name (*nam*), the word (*sabad*), the teacher (*guru*) and harmony (*hukam*). *Nam*, the divine Name,

Daily prayer

At the beginning of the *Granth* are a number of aphorisms composed by Guru Nanak and known as the *Japji*. The Japji consists of thirty-eight stanzas which, unlike the rest of the *Granth*, is said, not sung. Most Sikhs begin their day by reciting the first stanzas known as the *mool mantra*. It serves as a basic creed of Sikhism:

God is One,
He is the True Name,
The Maker and All-pervading Spirit
Fearing nothing, hating no one,
A Being beyond time,
Self-existent beyond birth,
Revealed by the grace of the Guru.

Before all things existed He was Truth,
In the beginning of all things He was
*   Truth,*
Today He is Truth, Nanak,
And Truth He will ever be.

and *sabad*, the divine Word, together express the whole nature and being of God. But humans, because of their nature, fail to recognize this presence, and so need a *guru*, or divine Preceptor. The divine Preceptor is the 'voice' of God mystically uttered within the human heart. Once awakened, the enlightened one looks around and within, to see *hukam*, the divine Order, or harmony. Salvation is then a matter of entering this pattern or harmony through regular, disciplined meditation on the divine Name. Ultimately this results in the devotee uniting with the divine harmony and the wheel of transmigration stops.

The community develops

Before his death Guru Nanak appointed a disciple to succeed him. And from that time, for more than a

A Sikh wedding in London. Marriage is both a social and spiritual union.

century and a half, leadership in the Sikh community was exercised by a succession of gurus. The tenth of these, Guru Gobind Singh (1666–1708), brought the line to an end and transferred authority to the community (*Khalsa Panth*) and the scripture (*Guru Granth*). Today, it is the scripture which is most important.

The Sikh community evolved between the time of Nanak and that of Gobind Singh. Its identity was forged in the context of the cultural, political and military development of the Punjabi people. The community struggled for survival in the face of Muslim Mughal emperors, it was incorporated into the community of the martial Jat caste, and then exposed to the Sakti (power) culture of the Shivalik hills area. The beards, turbans and martial valour commonly

Quotes from the Scriptures

There's no limit to God's praise, to His glorification no limit.
There's no limit to His works, to His giving no limit.
We cannot limit Him by our seeing or by our hearing.
We cannot know the limit of the secret of His heart.
We cannot know the limit of His created world.
We cannot know the limit of His own accepted limits.
How many cry out to know His limits?
But His limits cannot be discerned.
This limit no one can know.
The more that is described the more remains.
Great is the Lord, His throne is exalted.
Higher than the highest is His Name.
If anyone were to be as highly exalted as He,
Then he would know His exaltation.
But God alone knows how great He is.
Nanak, what we receive is the result of Grace.

Make contentment thine earrings, spiritual endeavour thy begging bowl and wallet, and meditation thy sacred ash.
Wear death like sackcloth, in manner of life let thy body be that of a virgin and faith in God be thy staff.
Let communion with all men be thy holy order, control of the mind means control of the world.
Hail, Hail to Him!
The First, the Pure, the One without beginning, the indestructible, from age to age retaining the same vesture.

A strong identity and sense of community is characteristic of Sikhs wherever they are in the world. This picture is of the inaugural celebrations of a Sikh temple in Kenya.

Festivals

Balsakhi The New Year and spring harvest, adapted from Hinduism, marked by an animal fair at Amritsar.

Divali The Hindu New Year, adapted by Sikhs for assembly in the gurdwaras.

Hola Mohalla Guru Gobind Singh adapted the Hindu Holi to give it a martial flavour; today it is marked by fairs and carnival processions.

Ceremonies

Naming When the mother has recovered after childbirth, the family visits the gurdwara to give thanks and name the child.

Marriage This is not just a social contract but a spiritual union. It is both a social and religious occasion.

Cremation Normally held the day after death; a family occasion, marked by readings from the scripture.

Initiation At puberty young Sikhs enter the Khalsa, or community; boys add *Singh* and girls *Kaur* to their surnames.

associated with Sikhism today are marks of this evolution. The climax came with the setting up of the Khalsa brotherhood, probably by Guru Gobind Singh in 1699. Members of the brotherhood had to accept baptism and a new code of discipline which included the Five Ks and a set of prohibitions.

One small dissenting group within Sikhism—the *sahaj-dhari*—does not honour the code in its fulness but claims to follow the teachings of the gurus in their pristine purity. If, in modern society, Sikhs abandon the externals of their faith, they run the risk of being called 'fallen' by the orthodox.

In other ways, too, Sikhism stood out from the common culture. It encouraged the elimination of caste distinctions and affirmed the equality of women. Concerning women, Guru Nanak is said to have observed: 'How can she be called inferior who begets kings?'

8

PARSISM

Parsism today seems a mixture of unrelated elements. Yet down the years, the influence of its founder, Zoroaster, has been enormous.

Parsis honour fire as a symbol of Ahura Mazda. The fire is kept in a fire temple where it is lovingly attended.

On the extreme edge of the western Iranian desert, in and around Bombay in India, in East Africa, and in many of the major cities of the world are pockets of a small community totalling no more than 120,000 members worldwide. They are the Parsis, or 'Persians', followers of the great Persian prophet, Zoroaster. From the eighth century onwards, in the face of Muslim persecution, the majority of them have fled from Iran to tolerant India and beyond.

Zoroaster

Zoroaster ('Zarathustra' in Persian) is commonly believed to have lived during the sixth century BC, a period remarkable for its prophetic endeavour and spiritual enlightenment. Modern scholars, however, tend towards a much earlier date, somewhere in the period 1500–1000 BC.

Zoroaster called for righteous-

Scriptures

The Parsi scriptures, known as the *Avesta*, are very varied, and arose over a vast period of time.

Yasna Mainly liturgical texts recited by the priest during rituals. They contain the *Gathas*, 17 songs attributed to Zoroaster and reckoned to be the oldest part.

Vendidad Mainly liturgical texts dealing with purification rites and the punishment of offenders.

Yashts Hymns of praise and prayers of the laity.

ness and allegiance to Ahura Mazda, the 'Wise Lord'. But he also believed in various good and evil spirits, particularly Angra Mainyu, the 'Evil Spirit', whom he appeared to give equal status with the Wise Lord. Both are eternal. This is why Parsism is often considered dualistic—believing in two opposing,

Parsis dispose of their dead in secluded buildings known as Towers of Silence.

Festivals

Ghambars Six seasonal festivals, including New Year, celebrated with services and feasts.

Farvardega Days in memory of the dead, marked by taking sandalwood to the temples and flowers to the temples of silence.

Jashans Anniversaries, for example in praise of Zoroaster.

and equally balanced, forces of good and evil in the world. Yet, because he did not believe that matter was essentially bad, Zoroaster taught that in the end Good would triumph over Evil. This is why Parsism claims to be monotheistic—believing in one Almighty God.

Moreover, humankind has a part to play in the triumph of Good over Evil: because Ahura Mazda created the world in order to help him overcome Angra Mainyu, humankind is constantly summoned to combat evil. So Parsis are seekers of the 'Good Life'—'good thoughts, good words and good deeds'.

Living the Good Life

Good deeds will be rewarded and bad deeds punished. The injustices and inequalities of this world will be set right in the next. For Parsis believe firmly in life after death, the coming of a Saviour, a day of judgment, a bodily resurrection and the salvation of all humankind to praise God for ever.

Because Parsis pursue the 'Good Life', Parsism is a highly moral religion and Parsis are renowned for their intelligence, integrity, industriousness, and philanthropy, and their contributions to commerce, industry, education and social work. Because Zoroaster's teaching most probably influenced Judaism (and therefore Christianity and Islam indirectly), especially during the period of Jewish exile in Babylon, and particularly concerning belief in life after death, Parsism has abiding significance and relevance for the contemporary world.

Ritual and tradition

But Parsism also owes much to the popular religion of ancient Iran. And so today, while reformists stress the importance of monotheism and morality, orthodox Parsis lay strong emphasis on ritual and tradition, for example, purification, worship and sacrifice. They pray at the five divisions of the day and ritualize all the great moments of life: birth, puberty, marriage, child-bearing and death. As part of their daily dress they wear a sacred thread, reminding them of their scriptures, and a shirt, symbolizing their religion, both received at initiation. Their priests, in addition, wear white robes and turbans. They are a distinctive people. They do not seek to win others to their faith because they believe each person should follow the religion into which he was born.

63

9

JUDAISM

Judaism is the religion of a nation—God's chosen people. Yet for more than half their history, the Jews have had no homeland.

Jerusalem's Wailing Wall, the remains of the temple destroyed in AD 70, is a place of pilgrimage for Jews.

Judaism is the religion of the Jewish people. There are 12 million Jews in the world, 6 million in the USA, 2 million in Israel, and 4 million dispersed throughout the world, many of them in Russia and Eastern Europe. In the holocaust of 1939–45, 6 million Jews were annihilated in the concentration camps of Nazi Germany, as Hitler's Gestapo sought to 'purify' the race.

In the aftermath of war, in 1948, the tiny state of Israel was born. It was created to secure a permanent homeland for Jews. Israel's short history has been one of remarkable economic achievement, and of painful struggle—for recognition, identity and survival. The 'Jewish story', their early history, is told in the Hebrew Bible, in particular in the *Pentateuch*, known as the Five Books of Moses, or the Torah (Law).

The patriarchs, Abraham, Isaac and Jacob, are revered as the founders of the Jewish people. In their daily prayers, Jews claim to be 'children of Abraham', the friend of God, and their nation is called Israel—the name God gave to Jacob.

Abraham crossed from Mesopotamia is about 1800 BC to settle in Canaan, 'the promised land'—later known as Palestine. In time of famine the twelve sons of Jacob took refuge in Egypt, where they later became slaves.

Then, probably about 1250 BC, their descendants, the Hebrews, were led out of Egypt by Moses. This was the *exodus*. On the way, on the top of Mount Sinai, the God of the patriarchs, now known as 'Yahweh', made a covenant with Israel. It was enshrined in the words of the Ten Commandments, engraved by Moses on stone tablets, and sealed with the blood of animal sacrifice. The God of Israel revealed himself as the God of history: not simply a tribal deity or nature spirit, but the Creator in control of his world. From that time on, Israel's national identity and its religion have been indissolubly linked.

Moses himself did not enter the promised land. It was his successor, Joshua, and the Judges (later leaders raised up by God) who moved into the land in which the people settled.

Longing for Zion (Jerusalem)

By the rivers of Babylon we sat and wept
when we remembered Zion.
There on the poplars
we hung our harps,
for there our captors asked us for songs,
our tormentors demanded songs of joy;
they said, 'Sing us one of the songs of Zion!'
How can we sing the songs of the Lord while in a foreign land?
If I forget you, O Jerusalem, may my right hand forget its skill.
May my tongue cling to the roof of my mouth
if I do not remember you,
if I do not consider Jerusalem my highest joy.

PSALM 137:1–6

The Ten Commandments
given to Moses on Mount Sinai

Then God spoke all these words:

I am the Lord your God, who brought you out of the land of Egypt, out of the house of slavery; you shall have no other gods before me.

You shall not make for yourself an idol, whether in the form of anything that is in heaven above, or that is on the earth beneath, or that is in the water under the earth. You shall not bow down to them or worship them; for I the Lord your God am a jealous God, punishing children for the iniquity of parents, to the third and the fourth generation of those who reject me, but showing steadfast love to the thousandth generation of those who love me and keep my commandments.

You shall not make wrongful use of the name of the Lord your God, for the Lord will not acquit anyone who misuses his name.

Remember the Sabbath day, and keep it holy. Six days you shall labour and do all your work. But the seventh day is a Sabbath to the Lord your God; you shall not do any work—you, your son or your daughter, your male or female slave, your livestock, or the alien resident in your towns. For in six days the Lord made heaven and earth, the sea, and all that is in them, but rested the seventh day; therefore the Lord blessed the Sabbath day and consecrated it.

Honour your father and your mother, so that your days may be long in the land that the Lord your God is giving you.

You shall not murder. You shall not commit adultery. You shall not steal. You shall not bear false witness against your neighbour.

You shall not covet your neighbour's house; you shall not covet your neighbour's wife, or male or female slave, or ox, or donkey, or anything that belongs to your neighbour.

When all the people witnessed the thunder and lightening, the sound of the trumpet, and the mountain smoking, they were afraid and trembled and stood at a distance, and said to Moses, 'You speak to us, and we will listen; but do not let God speak to us, or we will die.' Moses said to the people, 'Do not be afraid; for God has come only to test you and to put the fear of him upon you so that you do not sin.' Then the people stood at a distance, while Moses drew near to the thick darkness where God was.

EXODUS 20:1–21

They were in turn succeeded by a line of kings. The first three, Saul, David and Solomon, ruled Israel. Their successors ruled the divided kingdoms of Israel and Judah.

But Palestine, at the crossroads of East and West, was to be occupied in turn by Persia, Greece and Rome. Time after time her people were sent into exile, first to Babylon in the sixth century BC and from the second century AD onwards, to the four corners of the earth. Yet, conscious of being God's chosen people, they retained their racial, cultural and religious identity wherever they went and whatever they suffered.

revealed the Law.

The Law and obedience to it is therefore central to Judaism. It consists of 613 commandments (*mitsvot*)—248 positive and 365 negative. They are the expression of God's will and are therefore binding on the believing Jew. Jews have a duty to both God and humankind to lead a life in accordance with God's will. In so doing they bear witness to God and his purpose in the world. This is the essence of the idea of Israel's 'election'—their position as God's chosen people.

God and his law

The Torah does not argue for the existence of God: God is. He is one and eternal, creator and ruler of the universe. He is both all-powerful and all-loving. He created the world, including humankind, for the manifestation of his glory.

God makes himself and his purposes known to people through revelation. People respond and communicate with God through prayer and meditation. By means of this two-way process God gave humankind his Law, the Torah. To keep this Law is to hasten the establishment of God's kingdom (rule) on earth. A personal Messiah ('anointed one'), descended from David, Israel's greatest king, will herald the coming of the kingdom. So, in the scheme of salvation, the Jewish people play a special role, since it was to them that God

When he is thirteen years of age a Jewish boy becomes Bar Mitzvah, a 'son of the commandment'. From that time on he is held to be an adult, with all the responsibilities and privileges which this brings. In this Bar Mitzvah ceremony in Jerusalem the boy is carrying the Torah (the scrolls of the Law).

Prayer

A devout Jewish man prays three times a day—morning, afternoon and evening, either in his home or in the synagogue. When he prays he covers his head with an ordinary hat or a skull-cap (*yarmelka* or *kippah*). In the morning he wears a prayer-shawl (*tallit*) which has tassels or fringes at the four corners in obedience to the command found in the *Torah*. On weekdays he may also put on phylacteries (*tephillin*). These are black leather boxes containing four passages of scripture: Exodus 13:1–10 and 11–16; Deuteronomy 6:4–9 and 11:13–21. They are strapped to the forehead and left upper arm.

God and his world

According to the Jewish view of human society all persons are created in God's own image. All people are created equal. All have dignity. And so the Law commands respect for all. It also commands special care of the under-privileged—the sick, the widow, the orphan, the stranger, the distressed, the captive and the poor. This is emphasized through constant reference to Israel's own history: for example, as God's people were themselves 'strangers' in Egypt so they must be hospitable to strangers.

According to the Jewish view of human nature, all people are created free, with the ability to

Jewish families gather together for the Sedar, the home service of Passover. On the table are unleavened cakes, a shankbone of mutton, bitter herbs, paste made from apples, almonds, cinnamon and other spices, raisins, and salt water all to commemorate Israel's slavery in Egypt. The story of the slavery from which God delivered them is recounted, psalms sung, and food and wine shared.

choose between good and evil, and without the 'inheritance' of a burden of sin. And the world in which people are placed is a good world, created by God for the benefit of humankind. People must therefore enjoy its bounty and use its gifts both for the betterment of humankind and the service of God. Unlike Indian religion, therefore, Judaism is a world-affirming and not a world-denying faith. Salvation is to be achieved in and through this world. Thus, although Jews believe in the resurrection of the dead and the immortality of the soul, they pay far more attention to living life well here and now than preparing for the life to come.

The home

The centre of Jewish religious life is the home—even more than the synagogue. Jews lay great emphasis on the family and family relationships, and so many Jewish festivals are family festivals. Most notable is the weekly Sabbath.

Sabbath means 'rest', and 'the Sabbath' is a weekly day of rest from work and a festival of religious and family significance. The Jewish day begins and ends at sunset, so the Sabbath, which falls on Saturdays, begins on Friday evening.

Before sunset, the woman of the house kindles the 'Sabbath lights'. As she does so, she prays for God's blessing on her work and her family. The male members of the household may be with her, or they may be attending the synagogue.

The sabbath table is spread with a clean cloth and laid with two loaves and a cup of wine. Before the evening meal, the husband chants the praise of a virtuous wife and recites verses from the Bible about creation and the Sabbath rest. He then takes the cup of wine and blesses it in the name of God. He also blesses the bread, taking his portion of wine and bread before handing them round.

Jews of 'East' and 'West'

The majority of Jews throughout the world today are descendants either of the Ashkenazim or the Sephardim. The Ashkenazim came from central Europe, notably Germany ('Ashkenaz' means Germany) and France, and later moved to Poland and Russia. Ashkenazic Jews developed Yiddish (medieval German) as their language. Around it they produced a rich culture in art, music and literature.

Sephardic Jews ('Sepharad' means Spain) created the language of Ladino (a vernacular Spanish). Before being driven from Spain in the Inquisition of 1492, the Sephardim became closely involved with the Muslim world. This enabled them to develop a unique intellectual culture. The wide difference in cultural background between the Ashkenazim and Sephardim is especially evident in Israel today where each supports its own chief rabbi.

Divisions of Jewry

Orthodox This is the strictly traditional Judaism which accepts the Law and rabbinic authority.

Progressive This is represented by two movements. *Liberal Judaism* arose in continental Europe out of the eighteenth-century Enlightenment. It stressed biblical criticism, and emphasized the ethical and generally applicable aspects of Judaism over against the ritualistic and limited. *Reform Judaism* continues this tendency. It welcomes the methods of historico-critical research and plays down the observance of ritual. It also plays down the 'particularist' or

'nationalist' elements of Judaism—the hope of a return to Zion, the restoration of the sacrificial system and the coming of a personal Messiah.

Conservative This branch originated in the nineteenth century, especially in America, and steers its way between Orthodox and Progressive. It pleads for modification of ritual but accepts rabbinic tradition.

Mystical This is represented by two movements. The *Kabbalah* emerged in thirteenth-century Spain and emphasizes union with God through meditation and

contemplation. The *Hasidim* emerged from eighteenth-century Eastern Europe and emphasizes communion with God through enthusiastic prayer.

Zionist Cutting across all other divisions, Zionism is a nationalist movement, with spiritual overtones. It arose out of the persecutions of nineteenth-century Eastern Europe, stressed Jewish nationhood as well as peoplehood and culminated in the return to the land of Israel.

The synagogue

Synagogue means 'assembly'. It is the centre of public worship and social life for the Jewish community. Jews gather in the synagogue for Sabbath services held on Friday evening and Saturday morning.

The building may be square or oblong. At the end facing Jerusalem is the Ark, containing the scrolls of the Law. Pews are arranged on three sides, placed so that the worshippers face the Ark. In front

of the Ark is a reading-desk (*bema*) from which prayers are said and the Law read. Normally during the service men wear hats or skull caps, and white prayer shawls around their shoulders; women wear hats but no shawls. In orthodox synagogues, women sit separately from men.

During the service, all members of the congregation rise to repeat the *shema* (which all Jews recite twice daily): 'Hear, O Israel: The Lord our God, the Lord is One; and

Key concepts

The medieval Jewish philosopher, Moses Maimonides (1135–1204), drew up thirteen articles of faith, which are generally considered to sum up the essentials of Jewish belief.

- The existence of the Creator
- His unity
- His incorporeality (God is spirit)
- His eternity
- The obligation to serve and worship him alone
- The existence of prophecy
- The superiority of Moses to all the prophets
- The revelation of the Law to Moses at Sinai
- The unchanging nature of the Law
- The omniscience of God (God is all-knowing)
- Retribution in this world and the next
- The coming of the Messiah
- The resurrection of the dead

Wherever ten or more Jewish men live near together, a synagogue can be formed. The worship, teaching and social functions of the synagogue hold the community together.

Congregations are served by teachers or lawyers (rabbis) who are chief officers of the synagogue, readers (chazzan) who read lessons and recite prayers and priests (cohen, descendants of the temple priests).

you shall love the Lord your God with all your heart, and with all your soul, and with all your might.' At the climax of the service the Ark is opened and the scroll of the Law is taken out and carried round the synagogue. The people bow as it passes each pew. First the priests and members of the priestly line (Levites), and then any layman, may stand up and read the Law.

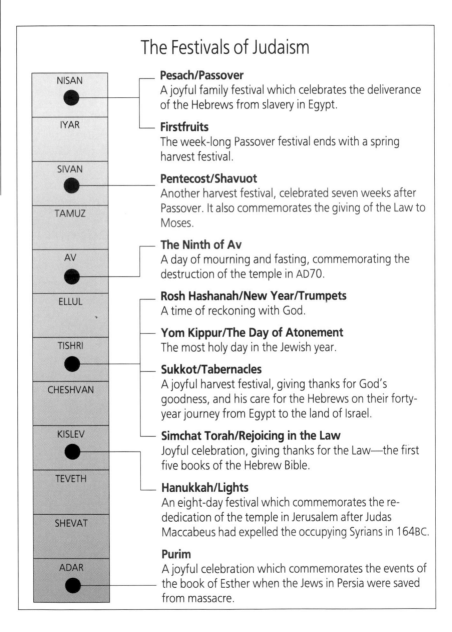

The Festivals of Judaism

NISAN

IYAR

SIVAN

TAMUZ

AV

ELLUL

TISHRI

CHESHVAN

KISLEV

TEVETH

SHEVAT

ADAR

Pesach/Passover
A joyful family festival which celebrates the deliverance of the Hebrews from slavery in Egypt.

Firstfruits
The week-long Passover festival ends with a spring harvest festival.

Pentecost/Shavuot
Another harvest festival, celebrated seven weeks after Passover. It also commemorates the giving of the Law to Moses.

The Ninth of Av
A day of mourning and fasting, commemorating the destruction of the temple in AD70.

Rosh Hashanah/New Year/Trumpets
A time of reckoning with God.

Yom Kippur/The Day of Atonement
The most holy day in the Jewish year.

Sukkot/Tabernacles
A joyful harvest festival, giving thanks for God's goodness, and his care for the Hebrews on their forty-year journey from Egypt to the land of Israel.

Simchat Torah/Rejoicing in the Law
Joyful celebration, giving thanks for the Law—the first five books of the Hebrew Bible.

Hanukkah/Lights
An eight-day festival which commemorates the re-dedication of the temple in Jerusalem after Judas Maccabeus had expelled the occupying Syrians in 164BC.

Purim
A joyful celebration which commemorates the events of the book of Esther when the Jews in Persia were saved from massacre.

The Jewish scriptures

Bible ('books') A collection of books written over a period of 1,000 years and given the status of scripture about AD 100.

Torah ('law') The first five books of the Bible, attributed to Moses.

Mishnah ('repetition') Ethical and ritual teaching based on the Bible, dating from the second century AD onwards.

Talmud ('study') In two versions, one Palestinian and one Babylonian, based on the Mishnah, with further reflections.

Religious observances

In addition, the religious life of a devout Jew is marked by prayer three times daily and the keeping of strict laws on diet, involving the declaration of all food as clean. As a sign of the covenant made between God and Abraham, all Jewish boys are circumcised eight days after birth. Traditionally, the ceremony took place in the home or in the synagogue, but nowadays, it usually takes place in hospital, in the presence of a rabbi.

CHRISTIANITY

Christianity offers the world today
a message concerned with changing both the
individual and society.

The cross is a universal symbol of Christianity.

Christians take their name from Jesus Christ. Jesus was born in Bethlehem, in Judea, sometime between 6 and 4 BC, to a devout Jewish couple named Mary and Joseph, descendants of King David. He grew up in Nazareth, in Galilee, and at the age of 30 was baptized in the River Jordan by a prophet called John the Baptist. John had been preaching and baptizing people as a mark of repentence for sins. He heralded the coming of one greater than himself.

After his baptism, Jesus gathered round him a band of twelve disciples (the 'apostles'), and went about the countryside preaching, teaching and healing the sick. He announced the coming of God's rule and declared the need for people to repent of their sins and believe the good news of God's kingdom. When, after many months together, Jesus asked his disciples who he was, their leader, Peter, declared 'You are the Christ' —the 'anointed one', the Messiah of Jewish expectation.

At the age of 33 Jesus was arrested, tortured and put to death by the Roman authorities, with the collaboration of Jewish secular and religious leaders, probably about AD 29–30. He died by crucifixion, a common but very painful method of execution. But he rose from the dead three days later, appeared to some women followers and his disciples on a number of occasions during the next 40 days, and then returned to his Father in heaven.

Christians therefore believe in a living Christ, not a dead hero. The crucifix and the cross have become symbols of the suffering Saviour and the risen Lord. Friday and Sunday, the day on which he died and rose, have become 'holy' days.

Who was Jesus?

Christians believe that Jesus Christ is both 'Son of God' and 'Son of Man'—fully human and fully divine and without sin. In him, the One God, Creator of heaven and earth, came down to human beings, in order to raise them to be with God. This is the *incarnation*, achieved through being conceived by the Holy Spirit in a woman who was a virgin. Jesus took on himself the limitations of human nature.

He also took responsibility for the sins of the human race, reconciling humankind with God, and God with humankind. This is the *atonement*, achieved through his death. But he died only to rise again to new life. This is the *resurrection*.

Those who believe in Jesus are not only saved from their sins but will be raised to new life when Jesus comes again. Meanwhile, through the Spirit of God living in them, they are guided and strengthened in their pilgrimage on earth.

The birth of the church

After Jesus had ascended to his Father in heaven, his followers gathered in Jerusalem to await the coming of the Spirit of God whom Jesus had promised. Ten days later, the Holy Spirit came, and Peter, leader of the twelve apostles, filled with new boldness and power, addressed the crowds. He told them that Jesus, whom they had crucified, and whom God had raised from the dead, was the promised Messiah, and called on them to turn from their sins and be baptized in his name. Three thousand responded to this first preaching of the Christian message and were baptized.

From Jerusalem the church spread outwards until, by the close of the century, it was strong in Asia Minor, Macedonia, Greece and Rome. The expansion was due largely to the efforts of Paul, the first great Christian missionary. Paul made known the good news about Jesus—the 'gospel'. He used to full advantage the widespread law and justice which resulted from the 'Roman peace', the ease of communication made possible by the Greek language, and the privileged position accorded to the Jewish religion.

And the churches which he founded in turn preached the gospel, so that by the end of the second century the church had spread throughout the Mediterranean world, into Egypt, North Africa and even France. Christianity was providing a real reason for living: life in this world and hope in a world to come.

Christians go through the waters of baptism (either by 'sprinkling' or by 'immersion') to symbolize dying and and rising with Christ and being born to new life. The early Christians probably confessed their faith at baptism in the words of the exclamation 'Jesus is Lord!' Since the fourth century, Christians in the West have used a creed approximating to the 'Apostles Creed' for the same purpose.

The church worldwide

Yet, success was not without cost. Persecutions were common. And they, more often than not, led to quarrels and disputes which divided and weakened the church, sometimes irretrievably.

But then, with the issue of the Edict of Milan by the Emperor Constantine in AD 313, persecutions ceased. Christianity was now officially tolerated and before long became the state religion. On the one hand, the church's alliance with the state had a high price: until that time Christians had been a persecuted minority; from now on it would be convenient to be a

Key beliefs

The Christian creeds express the essence of Christian belief. They fall into three sections, concerned with God, Jesus Christ and the Holy Spirit. The familiar 'Apostles' Creed' is used only in the Western church; the Nicene Creed, which follows, is used in the church worldwide, although the Eastern church omits the 'filioque' clause (in brackets).

We believe in one God,
the Father, the almighty,
maker of heaven and earth,
of all that is,
seen and unseen.

We believe in one Lord, Jesus Christ,
the only Son of God,
eternally begotten of the Father,
God from God, Light from Light,
true God from true God,
begotten, not made,
of one Being with the Father.
Through him all things were made.
For us and for our salvation
he came down from heaven;
by the power of the Holy Spirit
he became incarnate of the Virgin Mary,
    and was made man.
For our sake he was crucified under
Pontius Pilate;
he suffered death and was buried.
On the third day he rose again
in accordance with the Scriptures;
he ascended into heaven
and is seated at the right hand of the
    Father.
He will come again in glory
to judge the living and the dead,
and his kingdom will have no end.

We believe in the Holy Spirit,
the Lord, the giver of life,
who proceeds from the Father (and the
    Son),
With the Father and the Son he is
    worshipped and glorified.
He has spoken through the prophets.
We believe in one holy catholic and
    apostolic Church.
We acknowledge one baptism for the
    forgiveness of sins.
We look for the resurrection of the
    dead,
and the life of the world to come.

The Festivals of Christianity

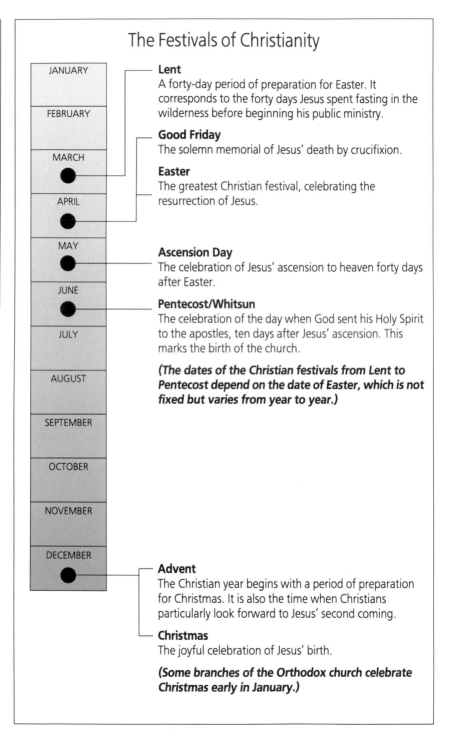

JANUARY	**Lent** A forty-day period of preparation for Easter. It corresponds to the forty days Jesus spent fasting in the wilderness before beginning his public ministry.
FEBRUARY	
MARCH	**Good Friday** The solemn memorial of Jesus' death by crucifixion.
	Easter The greatest Christian festival, celebrating the resurrection of Jesus.
APRIL	
MAY	**Ascension Day** The celebration of Jesus' ascension to heaven forty days after Easter.
JUNE	**Pentecost/Whitsun** The celebration of the day when God sent his Holy Spirit to the apostles, ten days after Jesus' ascension. This marks the birth of the church.
JULY	
AUGUST	*(The dates of the Christian festivals from Lent to Pentecost depend on the date of Easter, which is not fixed but varies from year to year.)*
SEPTEMBER	
OCTOBER	
NOVEMBER	
DECEMBER	**Advent** The Christian year begins with a period of preparation for Christmas. It is also the time when Christians particularly look forward to Jesus' second coming.
	Christmas The joyful celebration of Jesus' birth.
	(Some branches of the Orthodox church celebrate Christmas early in January.)

Christian for political, economic and social reasons. On the other hand, the alliance, first in the form of the Holy Roman Empire and later through national churches, resulted in the flowering of Western Christian culture – Christendom.

With the growth of the Holy Roman Empire developed the power of Christendom's chief religious leaders—the Pope of Rome and the Patriarch of Constantinople—and a struggle for supremacy. In 1054 the Pope excommunicated the Patriarch and the Patriarch did the same to the Pope. This formalized the separation of the Greek and Latin churches. They became the Eastern Orthodox and Roman Catholic churches respectively, and the break is known as the great East-West Schism.

Division and growth

Along with the rest of Europe, the church emerged from the darkness of the Middle Ages into the light of the Renaissance. But it found itself suddenly confronted with the stirrings of physical and spiritual freedom, and individual and national independence. In 1515–1516 in Germany, a young monk and scholar named Martin Luther became convinced, while preparing lectures on Paul's Letter to the Romans, that salvation could come only by faith, not by good works as the church was teaching. When challenged, he refused to submit to the Pope's authority. The Reformation had begun, the

The way

When his disciples asked him to teach them to pray, Jesus gave them this 'model' prayer:

Our Father in heaven,
hallowed be your name,
your kingdom come,
your will be done,
on earth as in heaven.
Give us today our daily bread.
Forgive us our sins
as we forgive those who sin against us.
Lead us not into temptation
but deliver us from evil.

Jesus summed up the Law in two short commandments. His summary is often called the Great Commandment:

The first commandment is this: 'Hear, O Israel, the Lord our God is the only Lord. You shall love the Lord your God with all your heart, with all your soul, with all your mind, and with all your strength.' The second is this: 'Love your neighbour as yourself.' There is no other commandment greater than these.

movement from which churches of the Protestant tradition spring.

Today, although in decline in Europe and North America, Christianity is rapidly gaining converts in Africa, South America and parts of Asia. It claims a world membership of 1,400 million.

Christian worship is collective as well as individual. Christians meet together to worship in all kinds of different ways and in all kinds of different situations. Cathedrals—such as this one at Notre Dame—are Christian churches on the grandest scale.

The community of believers

Christians worship together. Any group of Christians, meeting together regularly, whether in a home, a school hall or in the open air, is called a church. Special buildings for Christians to meet in have also come to be called churches.

Down the centuries, the building of churches has made an important contribution to the artistic and architectural heritage of the world. Churches are usually among the most beautiful and outstanding buildings in the villages, towns and cities of Europe, America and Australasia. Their towers and spires rise above the neighbouring houses, pointing people to God, and

the great ornamented cathedrals of the Western world are rivalled only by the great sculptured temples of southern India. One usually enters a church or cathedral by the west door. At the far end, directly facing the west door, is a table on which is placed a cross and two or six candles, or simply two vases of flowers. To left and right are the pulpit (where the sermon is preached) and lectern (where the Bible is read aloud).

Whether in a church building or elsewhere, Christians meet together to worship God, to learn together and to celebrate their beliefs. Shortly before he died, Jesus commanded his disciples to commemorate his death until his

Sacraments

A sacrament is an 'outward and visible sign of an inward and spiritual grace'. Catholics and Orthodox recognize seven sacraments: baptism, confirmation, the Eucharist, penance, extreme unction (anointing of the sick and dying), holy orders (bishops, priests and deacons), and marriage. Protestants generally recognize the two of these believed to be specifically commanded by Jesus: baptism and the Eucharist.

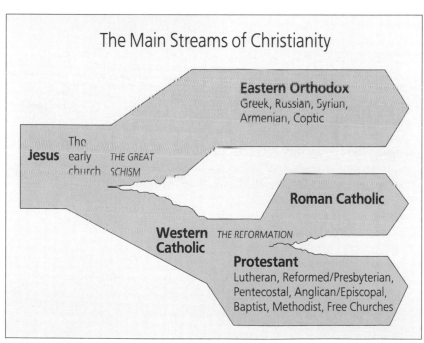

The Main Streams of Christianity

Eastern Orthodox
Greek, Russian, Syrian, Armenian, Coptic

Jesus The early church *THE GREAT SCHISM*

Roman Catholic

Western Catholic *THE REFORMATION*

Protestant
Lutheran, Reformed/Presbyterian, Pentecostal, Anglican/Episcopal, Baptist, Methodist, Free Churches

Scriptures

The Christian canon of scripture, known as the Bible, was finally agreed on between AD 170 and 220. It contains 39 books of Jewish scripture (the Old Testament) and 27 books of Christian scripture, (the New Testament). Some people add to these the Apocrypha, a collection of Jewish writings which formed part of the Greek version of the Jewish scriptures, but which were excluded from the accepted Hebrew canon.

The New Testament consists of four Gospels, the Acts of the Apostles, the letters of Paul, the general letters, and the Revelation of John. Christians believe that the Bible is the written Word of God, which bears witness to Jesus, the living Word (*Logos*).

Calendar

The main events in Jesus' life are celebrated in the festivals of the Christian church:

Advent Prepares for the coming of Christ (the Messiah).

Christmas Celebrates the birth of Jesus and is held on 25 December.

Lent A period of spiritual discipline leading up to Easter.

Easter Commemorates the death and resurrection of Jesus.

Ascension Celebrates Jesus' ascension into heaven; held 40 days after Easter.

Pentecost Marks the coming of the Holy Spirit; held on the fiftieth day after Easter.

return to earth at the end of the present age. Ever since that night, Christians have done this in the celebration known as the Mass, the Eucharist, Holy Communion or the Lord's Supper.

For churches of the Catholic and Orthodox traditions, this is the main service, often held daily. It is the main way in which the faithful receive help from God and feel his presence. Prayers are said, passages from the Bible are read and explained, hymns are sung, and bread and wine are consecrated to represent the body and blood of Christ. The priest then distributes the bread and the wine (or the bread only) to the faithful who gather

round the table.

In churches of the Protestant tradition, the emphasis is different. Holy Communion may be celebrated less frequently: in some fortnightly or monthly or only twice a year. The main way in which believers receive spiritual nourishment is through hearing the word of God and obeying it.

In the main service on Sundays the preaching of the 'Word of God' is of chief importance. Prayers are said, passages from the Bible are read, hymns are sung and then a sermon is preached. The preacher concludes with a call to the people to hear the word of the Lord.

Christians also worship

Christianity is a world faith. As it has spread, new believers have come from all sorts of backgrounds. The Christian Bible has been translated into almost 2,000 languages. Here, Kenyan Christians meet to worship.

individually. They experience God in private prayer and devotion as well as in corporate worship with other believers.

Service

But Christian worship involves serving people as well as God. Medical, educational and relief work has always been a vital part of Christian activity worldwide. Christianity is a world-affirming and not a world-denying religion. God created a good world. It was human beings who succumbed to temptation and introduced sin. Yet, God so loved the world that he sent a redeemer. And salvation is achieved through God's redeeming the world and not by humanity's renouncing it. For this reason Christians work for the physical as well as the spiritual well-being of mankind.

ISLAM

To the Muslim, Islam is life. It is submission to
Allah. And the natural implication is Allah's desire
to have all the world submit.

*Prayer and worship are central to Islam. The word 'muslim'
means 'one who lives his life according to God's will'. Islam
means 'submission to God'.*

Islam is the world's third great monotheistic religion. It sprang from the same root as the other two, Judaism and Christianity. 'Islam', an Arabic word, comes from a root meaning 'commitment' or 'surrender': Islam is a religion of submission. Its followers, 'Muslims', are 'those who commit themselves in surrender to the will of God (Allah).

Islam is also a religion which emphasizes success and therefore it is a militantly missionary religion. Conscious of a glorious past and powerful contemporary influence, Islam is set to conquer the world. Muslims believe that their faith meets all the spiritual and religious needs of humankind.

A Muslim creed

*O believers, believe in God and His Messenger
and the Book He has sent down on His messenger
and the Book which He sent down before.
Whoso disbelieves in God and His angels
and His Books, and His Messengers, and the Last Day, has surely gone astray into far error.*

QUR'AN IV.135

The Prophet

Islam traces its origin to the Prophet Muhammad who was born in the city of Mecca, Arabia, about AD 571. At that time a power vacuum existed between the two great empires of East and West, Persia and Byzantium. Mecca was a centre of the prosperous caravan trade between Southern Arabia and the Mediterranean.

Orphaned at an early age, Muhammad was looked after by a succession of relatives. Eventually a rich uncle sent him on trading excursions to the north where it is reported that he met Christians. At the age of 25, to his surprise, he was proposed to by a wealthy widow of 40 named Khadija. She bore him three daughters but no son.

In middle life, Muhammad began to show mystical traits and developed the habit of withdrawing to the hills for contemplation. On one such occasion, at the age of 40, he received a revelation calling him to denounce the paganism and polytheism of Mecca and preach the existence of one God, Allah. He was encouraged by his wife, but in the first ten years only a few others followed him. Some of these were prominent citizens, who are known as 'the Companions'.

Islam takes root

Then in AD 622, at the request of the citizens of nearby Medina, he left Mecca for Medina, accompanied by a few followers. This is the celebrated *hijra* or 'emigration', the event from which the Muslim calendar begins. Over the next few years Muhammad organized his followers and the citizens of Medina as a religious and political community and began to attack the trade caravans from Mecca. Meanwhile, he had expelled most of the Jewish tribes, whom he had hoped to win, and gradually incorporated the Bedouin tribes of Western and Central Arabia into the Muslim community. In 630, he massed an attack against Mecca, which finally surrendered. Muhammad immediately set about eliminating the polytheists. He rededicated the ancient sanctuary of the Ka'aba to Allah, making it the central shrine of pilgrimage for Muslims. It remains so to the present day.

Quotations from the Scriptures

The Star Revealed at Mecca

In the name of Allah, the Beneficent, the Merciful.
By the Star when it setteth,
Your comrade erreth not, nor is deceived:
Nor doth he speak of (his own) desire.
It is naught save an inspiration that is inspired,
Which one of mighty powers hath taught him,
One vigorous: and he grew clear to view
When he was on the uppermost horizon.
Then he drew nigh and came down
Till he was (distant) two bows' length or even nearer,
And He revealed unto His slave that which He revealed.
The heart lied not (in seeing) what it saw.
Will ye then dispute with him concerning what he seeth?
And verily he saw him yet another time
By the lote-tree of the utmost boundary,
Nigh unto which is the Garden of Abode.
When that which shroudeth did enshroud the lote-tree,
The eye turned not aside nor yet was overbold.
Verily he was one of the greater revelations of his Lord.
Have ye thought upon Al-Lâte and Al-'Uzzâ
And Manât, the third, the other?
Are yours the males and His the females?
That indeed were an unfair division!
They are but names which ye have names, ye and your fathers, for which Allah hath revealed no warrant. They follow but a guess and that which (they) themselves desire. And now the guidance from their Lord hath come unto them.
Or shall man have what he coveteth?
But unto Allah belongeth the after (life), and the former.

SURA 53.1–25

TRANSLATED BY MOHAMMED MARMADUKE PICKTHALL

The next two years were spent consolidating the tribes of Arabia. Then, suddenly, in 632, Muhammed died without naming a successor. He was succeeded by a series of caliphs ('successors'), the first two of whom were the Companions, Abu Bakr and 'Umar.

The Qur'an and the Hadith

Soon after the death of Muhammad, the revelations which he had received were put together from oral and written sources to form the *Qur'an* ('recitation'). The authorized version, written in incomparable classical Arabic, was prepared about AD 650 under the third caliph, 'Uthman. Muslims believe that the Qur'an is the infallible Word of God sent down from heaven and that nothing has changed it. Simply to recite it in the original, whether understood or not, brings the Muslim grace (*baraka*).

A Saudi Arab boy reading the Qur'an, the sacred book of Muslims.

Next in importance to the Qur'an is the *Hadith* ('tradition'), which is the record of the life and activities of Muhammed and the early Muslim communities. It contains the *Sunna* ('example') of the Prophet, the standard which all Muslims should follow. Qur'an and Sunna have combined to form the *Shari'a* ('law'), and extraordinarily comprehensive guide to life and conduct.

God and his angels

The doctrine of God is central to the Qur'an. Like the Bible, the Qur'an assumes the existence of God and

Jesus in the Qur'an

Islam believes in Prophets sent by God to preach the unity of God and to warn men of the Judgment. Several of the Prophets rank above others, particularly Adam, Noah, Abraham, Moses, Jesus and Muhammad According to the Qur'an, Jesus was born of Mary but did not die. Instead, someone died in his place and God raised Jesus to himself. For death would have been failure, and a Prophet cannot be allowed to fail. To believe that Jesus was God would be the great sin of 'ascribing partners to God'.

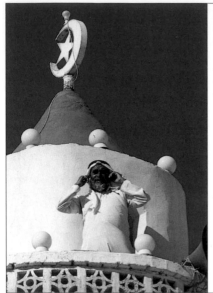

Muslims are called to prayer at fixed hours by the muezzin, who then leads them in prayer. There are five prayer times, each preceded by obligatory ritual washing—dawn, midday, mid-afternoon, sunset and night.

All around the world Muslims join together in direction (facing towards Mecca) and in intention as they pray as a single body.

does not argue for it. God is one and unique, with neither partners nor equals. He is good and all-powerful, as can be seen from natural phenomena, which are 'signs' of God's power and bounty. However, although the Qur'an affirms that God rules over all, it also teaches that humankind has responsibility.

The Qur'an states that to God belong the most beautiful names and as Islam developed, the names of God came to play an important role. Ninety-nine names emerged and these are recited whilst using a 'rosary'. Among the most important are: 'the Great', 'the Merciful', 'the Disposer' and 'deity'.

The Qur'an strongly affirms the existence of angels, who are God's messengers. But it also believes in the existence of spiritual beings called *jinn*. These were created from fire and not from clay like human beings, and their purpose is to serve or worship God. Rebellious *jinn* are called demons. The chief demon is Iblis or Satan, whom God allows to tempt people to evil. Alongside the angels God appoints prophets to be his messengers, beginning with Adam, through Abraham to Jesus, and ending with Muhammad, the 'seal' of the prophets.

Life now and the last day

Next in importance to the doctrine of God in the Qur'an is the doctrine of the Last Judgment. On the last day the whole of humanity will be raised to life and will appear before God to be judged and to be assigned

The Five Pillars of Islam

- Confession of Faith (*shahada*)
  'There is no God but God, and
  Muhammad is the Prophet of God.'
  A recital of this confession may be
  enough to win a new convert.

- Prayer (*salat*) Muslims pray five
  times daily—at daybreak, noon,
  mid-afternoon, after sunset, and
  early in the night—alone, in
  company, or in the mosque.
  Particularly important for adult
  males is the congregational prayer
  at noon on Fridays, which usually
  includes a sermon.

- Fasting (*Ramadan*) During the
  month of Ramadan Muslims must
  not eat or drink, smoke or have
  sexual relations between dawn and
  sunset.

- Almsgiving (*zakat*) Muslims must
  give two and a half per cent of their
  income and certain kinds of
  property to charity.

- Pilgrimage (*hajj*) A Muslim is
  required to go to Mecca once in his
  lifetime.

to Paradise or Hell, depending on
whether their deeds have been
mainly good or mainly bad.

The Qur'an also contains
regulations for the life of the
Muslim community. It deals with
religious and social behaviour such
as prayer, almsgiving, fasting,
pilgrimage, marriage, adultery and
divorce, inheritance, food and drink,
usury and slavery.

A law for life

During the first and second
centuries of Islam, its theologians
and lawyers worked out the
Shari'a, the law of Islam. This rests

Jihad

Jihad or 'holy war' literally means
'struggle'. On the one hand, the
Qur'an calls believers to 'fight in the
Way of God' against those who fight
against them—though it forbids them
to commit aggression. On the other
hand, it also recommends that those
who 'ascribe partners to God' (so
denying the unity of God) should be
killed and Jews and Christians made to
pay tribute unless they submit.

on four foundations: first, the Qur'an; second, the Sunna of the Prophet; third, analogy (*qiyas*) (deriving a new law from an existing law in the first two); and fourth, consensus of opinion (*ijma*) by means of interpretation (*ijtihad*) by experts (*ulama*) on behalf of the whole community.

A fixed code of behaviour developed which all Muslims were to follow. And 'unlike any other system in the world today the Shari'a embraces every detail of

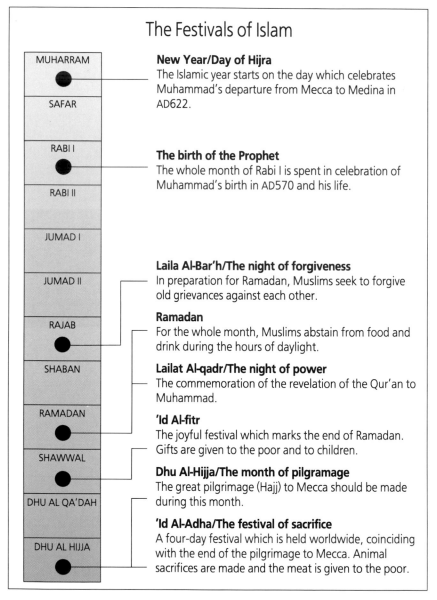

The Festivals of Islam

MUHARRAM	**New Year/Day of Hijra** The Islamic year starts on the day which celebrates Muhammad's departure from Mecca to Medina in AD622.
SAFAR	
RABI I	**The birth of the Prophet** The whole month of Rabi I is spent in celebration of Muhammad's birth in AD570 and his life.
RABI II	
JUMAD I	
JUMAD II	**Laila Al-Bar'h/The night of forgiveness** In preparation for Ramadan, Muslims seek to forgive old grievances against each other.
RAJAB	**Ramadan** For the whole month, Muslims abstain from food and drink during the hours of daylight.
SHABAN	**Lailat Al-qadr/The night of power** The commemoration of the revelation of the Qur'an to Muhammad.
RAMADAN	**'Id Al-fitr** The joyful festival which marks the end of Ramadan. Gifts are given to the poor and to children.
SHAWWAL	**Dhu Al-Hijja/The month of pilgramage** The great pilgrimage (Hajj) to Mecca should be made during this month.
DHU AL QA'DAH	**'Id Al-Adha/The festival of sacrifice** A four-day festival which is held worldwide, coinciding with the end of the pilgrimage to Mecca. Animal sacrifices are made and the meat is given to the poor.
DHU AL HIJJA	

human life, from the prohibition of crime to the use of the toothpick, and from the organization of the State to the most sacred intimacies—or unsavoury aberrations—of family life. It is "the science of all things, human and divine", and divides all actions into what is obligatory or enjoined, what is praiseworthy or recommended, what is permitted or legally indifferent, what is disliked or deprecated and what is forbidden.' For the Muslim there is no distinction between personal and communal, religious and secular, sacred and profane, spiritual and material. This often makes it difficult for the West to understand and appreciate the Islamic and Arabic worlds, and vice versa. Muslims believe overwhelmingly in a Creator, whose purpose for the world is all-embracing; human beings take part in his creative activity as his representatives on earth.

Discovering God's will

Islam is divided into two groups, *Sunni* and *Shi'ite*. The major difference between them is the way in which divine guidance is discovered. Sunni Muslims (who make up about 90 per cent of the total) take their stand on the consensus of the community making known the Sunna of the Prophet. Shi'ite Muslims look instead to inspired teachers or Imams. The Imams were descendants of Ali, the nephew and adopted son of the Prophet, who possessed secret knowledge and special interpretation passed down from Muhammad himself.

Three main groups of Shi'ites survive. The Zaidis of the Yemen recognize a living series of Imams. The Twelve-Imam Shi'ites, who dominate in Iran, believe that the line ended with the twelfth Imam. The Seven-Imam Shi'ites, or Ismailis of India and East Africa,

Islamic law deals with all areas of life, including family life and dress codes as well as matters of civic concern. These women athletes from Iran are dressed according to traditional Islamic law.

Islamic communities can be found the world over. This picture is of Beja Nomads from Sudan who follow the Muslim faith.

Pilgrimage to Mecca Hajj

The fifth of the five pillars of Islam is the pilgrimage to Mecca and its vicinity. Pilgrimage is to be fulfilled once in a lifetime if at all possible.

Here in Mecca are to be found the most holy places of Islam: places associated with Muhammad and the Companions, with the giving of the Qur'an, and with the Prophet Abraham himself who, according to the Qur'an, built the Ka'aba assisted by his son Ishmael.

To visit Mecca at any time of the year has religious significance for Muslims. It is a Little Pilgrimage. But to visit Mecca in the twelfth month of the calendar—

dhu alhijja—is to participate in the Great Pilgrimage.

At this time pilgrims flock to the city wearing a simple garb of white cloth to signify a state of ritual purification. They gather in the Great Mosque and perform the first rite of pilgrimage— circumambulation around the Ka'aba. They then run seven times between two small hills, recalling the plight of Hagar and her son Ishmael who, according to Jewish, Christian and Islamic tradition, were saved from certain death by a spring of water which God caused to gush forth from the sands of the desert. According to Islamic

tradition this well is called *zamzam*, and pilgrims may draw holy water from it before journeying out of Mecca to Mount Arafat where the Pilgrimage reaches its climax as pilgrims 'stand' from midday to sunset in meditation before God.

Following this, pilgrims begin the return journey to Mecca, stopping overnight at Mazdalifa where each of them gathers pebbles. Then next day in the neighbouring village of Mina they throw the pebbles against three stone pillars recalling the moments in Abraham's life when he resisted Satan's temptations to disobey God. According

are the followers of the Aga Khan and believe that the line ended with the seventh Imam.

Both the Seven-Imam and the Twelve-Imam Shi'ites await the appearance of the 'hidden Imam' known as the Mahdi. Meanwhile, because they do not believe in the principle of consensus, their leading theologians, called Mujtahids, are considered spokesmen for the 'hidden Imam' and exercise extensive authority in religious, legal and even political matters. This is seen clearly in the activities of the Mullahs and Ayatollahs of contemporary Iran (many of whom claim to be descended from Ali). The Mujtahids take no account of the opinions of early lawyers but go back directly to general principles contained in the Qur'an, the Sunna and the Hadith.

to the Qur'an Abraham had been commanded by God to prepare his son Ishmael for sacrifice as a test of his obedience (islam). However, the child was ransomed 'with a tremendous victim' and, in joyful recollection of this act of divine mercy, the pilgrims offer the ritual sacrifice of sheep or camels, a ritual of which the Qur'an comments: 'their flesh and blood reach not to God, but your devotion reaches him'. And all over the world, for four days, Muslims join with the pilgrims at Mina for the Festival of Sacrifice which brings the Great Pilgrimage—Hajj—to an end. Thus they fulfil what Abraham is believed to have prayed at the Ka'aba: 'Our Lord! And make us submissive unto Thee, and of our seed a nation community submissive unto Thee, and show us our ways of worship, and relent toward us. Lo! Thou, only Thou, art the Relenting, the Merciful' (Qur'an, Sura 2.128).

The Ka'aba is the central point of the Muslim holy city of Mecca. It is a stone structure containing a black stone, probably a meteorite, dating from pre-Islamic Arabia. Every Muslim, if resources and circumstances permit, should once in a lifetime make the pilgrimage (hajj) to Mecca.

EPILOGUE

People have called themselves 'Christian' for many different reasons. And I can echo many of them in my own experience. But at heart, to be a Christian is to be a follower of Jesus Christ.

I am a Christian because my parents were Christians before me. I was born and brought up in an Irish village, where it was natural to believe and most unnatural not to. At home, I learned to pray at my mother's knee. At school, I listened to stories from the Bible and became aware of my Irish Christian heritage. At Sunday school, I mastered the catechism. In church, I discovered what it meant to worship God.

And throughout I learnt to observe and celebrate—with everyone else in the village—the significant moments of the Christian life and the great events of the Christian year. Baptisms, confirmations and holy communions, Christmas, Easter and Pentecost, all stand out as some of the most momentous and memorable occasions of childhood.

I am a Christian because as a teenager I made a conscious decision to follow Jesus. By means of what can be called a conversion experience I entered into a personal relationship with Jesus Christ as Saviour and Lord, receiving the forgiveness of sins and embarking

on a new life. I persisted as a Christian through adolescence.

From time to time, doubting the existence of God for intellectual reasons, I suspended belief for brief periods. Later, at college, I took as my motto Anselm's famous maxim: 'I do not seek to understand so that I may believe; but I believe so that I may understand. For I believe this also that "unless I believe, I shall not understand".'

I am a Christian despite the problem of pain. I experienced a time of acute personal suffering in my late twenties and it was then I realized that the Christian God is a God who himself entered into the suffering of the world, so as to redeem it. The cross, the crucifixion of Jesus Christ, is at the centre of Christianity.

I am a Christian because, encountering the world's other religions in Africa, I recognized in Jesus Christ the Word of God (the Logos), the light who enlightens every person who comes into the world. Religion is not only our search for God but rather God's finding of us. The Word became flesh and dwelt among us.

I am a Christian despite the fact that we live in a world full of sinful people and marred by unjust social structures. For Jesus came to initiate change: 'to bring good news to the poor, to proclaim liberty to captives and to the blind new sight, to set the downtrodden free, to proclaim the Lord's year of favour'.

A poem of the cross

The death and resurrection of Jesus is the central fact of Christianity. This hymn from Ireland sums up what his death means to the believer.

There is a green hill far away
  Outside a city wall,
Where the dear Lord was crucified,
  Who died to save us all.

He died that we might be forgiven,
  He died to make us good,
That we might go at last to heaven,
  Saved by his precious blood.

We may not know, we cannot tell
  What pains he had to bear,
But we believe it was for us
  He hung and suffered there

There was no other good enough
  To pay the price of sin,
He only could unlock the gate
  Of heaven, and let us in.

Oh dearly, dearly has he loved,
  And we must love him too,
And trust in his redeeming blood,
  And try his works to do.

MRS CECIL FRANCES ALEXANDER

Christ, the shield of God

The Christian follows Jesus Christ. The prayer of Saint Patrick, the patron saint of Ireland, expresses the desire for Christ to be in every part of his life.

Christ for my guardianship today...
Christ with me, Christ before me,
Christ behind me, Christ in me,
Christ under me, Christ over me,
Christ to right of me, Christ to left of me,
Christ in lying down, Christ in sitting, Christ in rising up,
Christ in the heart of every person who may think of me!
Christ in the mouth of every one who may speak to me!
Christ in every eye which may look on me!

I remain a Christian because I am convinced that in the person of Jesus Christ is to be found all the fulness of God, in his message is to be discerned hope for our world, and in his church is to be discovered the foretaste of true community.

95

GLOSSARY

Altar A raised flat-topped structure where offerings are made to the deity; the communion table in Christian churches.

Anthropology The study of humanity.

Church A group of Christian believers; the body of all Christians; a building designed for public worship.

Contemplation Concentration of the mind and soul upon God.

Creed A system or statement of belief; particularly a brief formal summary of Christian belief.

Deity A god or goddess; the nature or character of God.

Dualism The belief that reality consists of two basic principles, mind and matter; the theory that the universe has been ruled from its origin by two conflicting powers, one good and one evil, both existing as equally ultimate first causes.

Grace Help or assistance given by God to humanity, in order to inspire, strengthen or bring spiritual rebirth.

Hymn Songs of praise to God, especially Christian.

Image A representation or likeness of a person or thing.

Lectern A reading-desk, especially in a church.

Magic The art of using spells to influence events by supernatural means.

Meditation Deep reflection on spiritual matters, especially as a religious act.

Monism The belief that reality consists of only one basic substance.

Monotheism The belief that there is only one God.

Mosque A Muslim place of worship.

Mysticism A system of contemplative prayer and spirituality aimed at achieving direct intuitive experience of the supernatural or the divine.

Polytheism The worship of or belief in more than one god.

Prayer A personal communication or petition addressed to a deity.

Priest A person who acts as a mediator between God and humanity by administer-ing the sacraments, preaching, blessing, guiding, making offerings and so on.

Prophet A person who speaks by divine inspiration; especially one through whom God reveals himself and expresses his will.

Pulpit A raised enclosed platform from which the preacher delivers a sermon.

Rabbi The spiritual leader of a Jewish congregation; an early Jewish scholar.

Reincarnation The belief that at death the soul is born again into another body.

Ritual The rising again of the dead at the Last Judgment.

Sacrament An outward sign combined with a prescribed form of words and regarded as conferring some specific grace upon those who receive it, especially in Christianity.

Sacrifice The killing of an animal or person, the surrender of a possession, as an offering to a deity.

Scripture A sacred or authoritative book or piece of writing.

Shaman A medicine man or priest who controls the spirits, especially among the tribespeople of North America and northern Asia.

Shrine A place of worship kept holy because of its association with a sacred person or object.

Sociology The study of human societies.

Symbol Something that represents or stands for something else, usually by convention or association.

Synagogue An assembly or congregation of Jews meeting for religious observance or instruction; the building in which they meet.

Temple A building dedicated to the worship of the deity, especially in the ancient world, in India and in the East generally.

Theology The systematic study of the existence and nature of God; a particular branch of this study, for example, Christian theology.

Worship Religious devotion and respect, especially its formal expression.